HEINEM
Integrated upper intermediate

JAN BELL
SERIES EDITOR PHILIP PROWSE

Heinemann International
A division of Heinemann Educational Books Ltd
Halley Court, Jordan Hill, Oxford OX2 8EJ

OXFORD LONDON EDINBURGH
MADRID ATHENS BOLOGNA PARIS
MELBOURNE SYDNEY AUCKLAND SINGAPORE TOKYO
IBADAN NAIROBI HARARE GABORONE
PORTSMOUTH (NH)

ISBN 0 435 28232 8

© Jan Bell 1990

First published 1990

All rights reserved; no part of this publication may be reproduced, stored in a retrieval system, or transmitted in any form or by any means, electronic, mechanical, photocopying, recording, or otherwise, without the prior written permission of the publishers.

Text acknowledgements

Our thanks are due to the following for their kind permission to reproduce a text: British Heart Foundation, p14; Daily Express, 'Chris's 40-coke habit', 5 December 1989, p16; Daily Mirror, 'Dreams from A-Zzzz', 4 July 1989, p34; Daily Telegraph plc, 'A Quiet Secure life is goal for Children', 2 September 1988, p36; Dr Vernon Coleman, 'Dreams - we uncover your secrets' (extracts from Woman's Own, 19 June 1988), pp32/3; Good Housekeeping, 'Teenagers Now', April 1988, p38; Hertfordshire Herald and Post, (MMS Publications), 'The Perils of Smoking', p16; The Independent, 'Days of Hope and Fear' by Sandra Barwick, December 1986, p62; Just Seventeen, 'Take Four Girls', 31 January 1990, pp49/50 and 'Dear Diary', 27 July 1988, pp60/61; Living, 'Test your diet and see how healthy it is', July 1988, p12; Lonely Planet Publications, *Indonesia - a travel survival kit*, 1986, p43; More, 'Palm Reading', 5 October 1988, p21; 19, 'It's my life ...', July 1988, pp40/41; Observer Magazine, 'New ways to learn', by Professor Ted Wragg, 3 September 1989, pp52/3; Octopus Publishing Group, *The world's greatest psychics and mystics*, by Margaret Nicholas, 1986, p25; Murray Pollinger Literary Agents, 'Lamb to the Slaughter' by Roald Dahl from *Someone Like You*, Penguin Books, Harmondsworth, pp2, 3, 4, 5, 6, 8, 9; Random Century Group Ltd, 'Bribery and Corruption', by Ruth Rendell from *The New Girlfriend and Other Stories*, pp64, 65, 66, 67, 68, 69, 70; She, 'Memories of the future - psychic report', by Shelley Bovey, June 1989, p25 and 'Deathly Hush-ups', July 1988; Tess Lemmon, 'Zoos - are they justified?', Greenscene (the Vegetarian Society), pp57/8; Woman/IPC Magazines, 'Animals we might lose forever', 7 February 1989, pp62/3 and 'The amazing lives ...', 25 October 1988, pp22/3; Woman's Own, 'Another time another place', 6 November 1989 (from *Mystic Forces*, Sinclair Publishing Ltd), p24; Woman's Realm, 'What's in a doodle?', 29 November 1988, p30 and 'The holiday rep', 10 October 1989, from 'And they get paid for doing it', pp20/21.

Photograph acknowledgements

We would like to thank the following for permission to reproduce photographs:
Barnabys, p57; Camera Press Ltd, pp59/60; Christine Osborne, pp42, 46; Malvin van Gelderen, p37; Professor G A Gresham, p20; Solo Syndication, p22.

Illustrations by
Nancy Anderson pp 11, 18, 21
Barbara Crow pp 25, 26
Oxford Illustrators pp 30, 31, 32, 33
Anthony Sidwell p 44
Paul Slater p 9

Cover by Carrie Craig

Printed and bound in Great Britain by
Thomson Litho Ltd, East Kilbride, Scotland

Contents

Map of the Book
Introduction   1

UNIT 1   STORYTELLING

Lesson	1	'I've got something to tell you'	2
	2	'Don't make supper for me. I'm going out.'	5
	3	'Get the weapon and you've got the man.'	8

UNIT 2   HEALTH AND FITNESS

Lesson	4	You Are What you Eat	11
	5	'It'll Never Happen to Me!	14
	6	Confessions of Food and Drink Junkies	16

UNIT 3   EARNING A LIVING

Lesson	7	The Job or the Money	18
	8	Jobs with a Difference	20
	9	A Job or Family Life?	22

UNIT 4   THE UNEXPLAINED

Lesson	10	The Paranormal	24
	11	Out of Body Experiences	26
	12	Debating the Issue	28

UNIT 5   THE UNCONSCIOUS MIND

Lesson	13	The Unconscious Mind	30
	14	To Sleep	32
	15	... Perchance to dream	34

UNIT 6   YOUNG PEOPLE TODAY

Lesson	16	Hopes for the Future	36
	17	Teenagers Now	38
	18	A Question of Class?	40

UNIT 7   TROPICAL PARADISE?

Lesson	19	Describing places	42
	20	Selling Tourism	44
	21	The Future of the Island	46

UNIT 8   EDUCATION

Lesson	22	Describing Schools	49
	23	Discussing Lessons	52
	24	University Life	55

UNIT 9   PETS AND WILDLIFE

Lesson	25	A 'Good Day Out' at the Zoo?	57
	26	A Strange Obsession?	59
	27	The Animals We Might Lose Forever	62

UNIT 10   BRIBERY AND CORRUPTION

Lesson	28	Bribery	64
	29	... and Corruption	68
	30	Revenge!	70

Teacher's Notes   72
Key   76
Tapescripts   81

Map of the book

		TOPIC	SKILLS

UNIT 1 MURDER

LESSON			
1	'I've got something to tell you.'	The end of a marriage	**Reading:** for information, for interpretation, for detail **Vocabulary:** searching for equivalent words and expressions **Listening:** for detail **Speaking:** prediction of the story **Writing:** the next part of the story
2	'Don't make supper for me. I'm going out.'	A death	**Speaking:** Reading stories aloud, discussion/prediction, mini role-play **Reading:** for detail **Vocabulary:** using verbs in sentences **Listening:** ordering information, completing sentences **Writing:** completing a form, writing a police report
3	'Get the weapon and you've got the man.'	The murder enquiry	**Reading:** for interpretation, for information **Vocabulary:** word association connected to weapons/murder **Listening:** sentence completion **Speaking:** dialogue building, group discussion **Writing:** a newspaper report

UNIT 2 HEALTH AND FITNESS

4	You Are What You Eat	Food	**Vocabulary:** matching food to categories, vocabulary of cooking, finding equivalent meanings **Reading** doing a 'healthy diet' quiz, reading interviews about people's daily habits **Listening:** Finding the score to the 'healthy diet' quiz **Speaking:** discussion on food, mini roleplay, giving advice on a healthy diet, working out questions and interviewing people **Writing:** writing up an interview from notes
5	'It'll Never Happen to Me'.	heart problems	**Vocabulary:** matching verbs to categories, finding opposite meanings **Reading:** giving headings to paragraphs, (from a leaflet) reading a letter for gist **Listening:** open questions **Speaking:** discussion **Writing:** an informal letter of advice
6	Confessions of Food and Drink Junkies	addictions	**Speaking:** prediction from newspaper headlines, group discussion, roleplay in pairs, survey **Reading:** for information, correcting false information **Vocabulary:** finding similar expressions, explaining in other words, matching words and definitions **Listening:** gap filling **Writing:** report writing

UNIT 3 EARNING A LIVING

7	The Job or the Money	'Caring' professions	**Speaking:** Comparing advantages and disadvantages of jobs, describing daily routine, discussing jobs **Listening:** matching to pictures, completing a chart for information **Vocabulary:** explaining vocabulary, brainstorm area of 'nursing' finding equivalent words in text **Reading:** matching question to paragraph, re-ordering jumbled text, reading for information **Writing:** writing an article about someone's job
8	Jobs with a Difference	Unusual or 'glamorous' jobs	**Speaking:** discussing, questions, palm-reading, checking prediction **Listening:** for detailed information **Vocabulary:** matching jobs to categories, identifying adjectives that describe you
9	A Job or Family Life?	Work and marriage/ children	**Speaking:** discussion based on quotes/prediction, information exchange **Reading:** chart completion/note-taking **Writing:** preparing questions, taking notes

TOPIC　　　　　SKILLS

UNIT 4　THE UNEXPLAINED

LESSON

10	The Paranormal	Strange or unexplained happenings	**Reading:** for information, matching extracts to topics, specific information **Vocabulary:** finding equivalent meanings, matching vocabulary of the paranormal **Speaking:** group story prediction, story telling **Writing:** group story writing, writing a ghost story **Listening:** ghost story
11	Out of Body Experiences	Near death experiences	**Reading:** ordering a text matching headings to texts **Speaking:** discussion **Listening:** a radio phone-in, gap filling **Vocabulary:** finding equivalent words in the text **Writing:** a letter to a radio station
12	Debating the Issue	Can near death experiences really happen?	**Reading:** re-read the texts to get information **Listening:** for information **Speaking:** language of opinions/agreeing/disagreeing, discuss points in groups, give point of view **Writing:** planning a discursive essay, writing a discursive essay

UNIT 5　THE UNCONSCIOUS MIND

13	The Unconscious Mind	What doodles show about our personality	**Speaking:** a discussion of habits **Reading:** matching definitions to doodles, locating specific information in a text, finding information **Vocabulary:** nouns from adjectives and adjectives from nouns to describe personality, marking syllable stress, positive and negative connotation of adjectives **Listening:** listening to explanations of doodles, and matching **Writing:** a description of someone's personality
14	To Sleep ...	Sleeping positions Dreams	**Reading:** a quiz for discussion, matching explanations of sleeping positions to pictures, reading a text on sleep for information match explanations to predictions **Speaking:** discussion of quiz **Vocabulary:** adjectives and their connotations, vocabulary of sleep **Writing:** diary extracts
15	... Perchance to dream	What dreams can tell us about ourselves	**Reading:** give appropriate titles to paragraphs on dreams, match explanations to text **Vocabulary:** find equivalent words in the text **Listening:** make notes on people's dreams **Speaking:** roleplay in pairs, explaining dreams, discussion based on dreams interpretation

UNIT 6　YOUNG PEOPLE TODAY

16	Hopes for the Future	Ambitions	**Speaking:** predict from newspaper headlines, discuss and compare teenagers lifestyles, work out questions, interview teenagers **Reading:** check predictions, match questions to paragraphs **Vocabulary:** jumbled words, finding equivalents in text **Listening:** prediction, ordering topics, listening for information **Writing:** writing questions, writing a short text, comparing teenagers' lifestyles
17	Teenagers Now	lifestyles	**Reading:** an extract by a teenager, for detail **Speaking:** giving opinions on controversial issues, interviewing an old person **Listening:** interview with an old lady, selecting and ordering topics, making notes **Writing:** creative writing, on teenagers
18	A Question of Class?	Different lifestyles of two 19 year olds	**Speaking:** discussion of different areas, prioritising, information exchange, discussion on class differences, interview **Reading:** identify main topics in each paragraph, make notes **Vocabulary:** find equivalent expressions in text **Writing:** summary of interview

UNIT 7　TROPICAL PARADISE?

19	Describing places	Descriptions	**Speaking:** discussion on picture **Vocabulary:** match descriptive words to categories, describe own country using this vocabulary, collocate adjectives with nouns **Reading:** match

		TOPIC	SKILLS
			text-type description to text **Writing:** write extracts describing places in factual and persuasive style
20	Selling Tourism	A description of a holiday	**Listening:** note taking **Reading:** Comparing brochure details to holiday, note taking **Vocabulary:** adjectives of 'persuasion' compared to factual language **Writing:** a holiday brochure letter of complaint **Speaking:** presenting the holiday
21	The Future of the Island	The problems caused by tourism	**Speaking:** discussion of what causes a tourist resort to be 'spoiled', roleplay **Listening:** completing a gapped summary of a radio talk **Writing:** a summary of the meeting, as a newspaper report

UNIT 8 EDUCATION

22	Describing schools	Different kinds of schools Rules & regulations	**Vocabulary:** different kinds of schools, **Reading:** predicting completing a chart with notes **Speaking:** information exchange, discussion on schools, interviews, for and against discussion **Writing:** Writing a for and against essay
23	Discussing Lessons	Lessons and the school curriculum	**Listening**: school children talking, prediction of what they will say, note-taking, reaction to opinions **Speaking:** interview, discussion of different curriculum systems **Reading:** factual text, for information **Vocabulary:** matching words with definitions **Writing:** a comparison of different systems of education
24	University Life	Life at a university	**Reading:** matching topic to paragraph, reading for information agreeing/disagreeing with extracts **Vocabulary:** find equivalent words or expressions in text **Listening:** Discussion on university and gap filling **Speaking:** Discussion on university education **Writing:** Summary of interview on university life

UNIT 9 PETS AND WILDLIFE

25	A 'Good Day Out' at the Zoo?	Is it cruel to keep animals in a zoo?	**Vocabulary:** Zoo animals and where they come from **Speaking:** Discussion on animals, interviews **Listening:** interviews about zoos, gist listening, notes for and against **Reading:** a newspaper article for detail **Writing:** summary of interview
26	A Strange Obsession?	British obsession with animals	**Reading:** read short extracts and complete gapped summary, ordering information, based on magazine article, reading for detail **Speaking:** discussion on animals, 'if this person were an animal' discussion **Listening:** match descriptions to appropriate photograph **Vocabulary:** explain in other words, keeping a diary
27	The Animals We Might Lose Forever	Disappearing wildlife	**Speaking:** prediction from photos, discussion on animal exploitation **Reading:** locating information **Vocabulary:** word puzzle based on vocabulary in text **Writing:** a short extract about the future

UNIT 10 BRIBERY AND CORRUPTION

28	Bribery ...	A visit to an expensive restaurant	**Speaking:** discussion of food and restaurants, roleplay predicting end of story **Reading:** for information, prediction, summary completion **Vocabulary:** finding equivalent words, reading dictionary entries, a dialogue
29	... and Corruption	A moral dilemma	**Reading:** for detail, for interpretation **Listening:** correcting statements, guided dictation **Speaking:** acting out a dialogue, prediction from headlines **Writing:** a summary
30	Revenge!	Nicholas gets his revenge	**Speaking:** reading stories aloud, discussion roleplay **Reading:** for information **Vocabulary:** finding equivalent words in the text **Listening:** sentence completion, listening for detail and interpretation **Writing:** a news report

Introduction

This book is intended for good intermediate level students who have already got a basic knowledge of grammar. The aims of the book are to:

- expose students to a variety of authentic written and spoken language, and to give them confidence in coping with it.

- provide plenty of opportunities for oral fluency, from discussion activities to full-scale roleplays.

- extend students' range of vocabulary (particularly informal colloquial language) and develop vocabulary skills such as deducing from context.

- give opportunties for students to write creatively, and try out a variety of different text types.

- expose students to language in use, with opportunities to revise areas of grammar or functional language which may still be causing problems.

The book is organised around ten units; each unit is made up of three lessons which are based broadly on the same theme. These themes have been chosen as ones which are likely to interest and motivate the average learner, and which are generative in terms of useful vocabulary areas. The themes include such topics as the supernatural and young people today, and two of the units are based on (unadapted) modern short stories - one by Roald Dahl, and the other by Ruth Rendell. Most of the units do not have to be taught in any particular order, although obviously some of the lessons within a unit do link together quite closely, and the short story units do follow a logical sequence.

Most of the written texts, apart from the short stories, are taken from newspapers and magazines. This means that they are of wide general interest, as well as providing a largely informal kind of language. The recordings were nearly all done outside the studio, in order to provide plenty of exposure to natural spoken language, and a variety of accents. Teachers might like to use these recordings, together with the tapescripts, to do more work on features of connected speech, such as intonation or sentence stress.

The activities which accompany the reading and listening text follow the common methodological procedure of pre, while and post activities in order to help students to make sense of the texts, and develop strategies.

The units are genuinely integrated so that, for example, a reading text may lead naturally to a group discussion or a listening text might result in the students' writing a report or predicting the end of the story.

The focus is essentially on fluency and the global use of the language, rather than practising language items. However, the teacher's notes at the back of the book give ideas on which language items emerge naturally out of each lesson, and how they could be exploited in more detail.

There is also a tapescript of the listening texts at the back of the book so that students can do follow-up work on their own, and a key with the answers to all the activities.

UNIT 1 MURDER!

1 'I've got something to tell you.'

This is a story by the British author Roald Dahl about a young married couple called Patrick and Mary Maloney.

1 Read the first part of the story below and then answer the questions.

Lamb to the Slaughter

1. The room was warm and clean, the curtains drawn, the two table lamps alight - hers and the one by the empty chair opposite. On the sideboard behind her, two tall glasses, soda water, whisky. Fresh ice cubes in the Thermos bucket.

2. Mary Maloney was waiting for her husband to come home from work.

3. Now and again she would glance up at the clock, but without anxiety, merely to please herself with the thought that each minute gone by made it nearer the time when he would come. There was a slow smiling air about her, and about everything she did. The drop of the head as she bent over her sewing was curiously tranquil. Her skin - for this was her sixth month with child - had acquired a wonderful translucent quality, the mouth was soft, and the eyes, with their new placid look, seemed larger, darker than before.

4. When the clock said ten minutes to five, she began to listen, and a few moments later, punctually as always she heard the tyres on the gravel outside, and the car door slamming, the footsteps passing the window, the key turning in the lock. She laid aside her sewing, stood up, and went forward to kiss him as he came in.

5. 'Hullo, darling,' she said.
   'Hullo,' he answered.

6. She took his coat and hung it in the closet. Then she walked over and made the drinks, a strongish one for him, a weak one for herself; and soon she was back again in her chair with the drink, and he in the other, opposite, holding the tall glass with both his hands, rocking it so the ice cubes tinkled against the side.

7. For her, this was always a blissful time of day. She knew he didn't want to speak much until the first drink was finished, and she, on her side, was content to sit quietly, enjoying his company after the long hours alone in the house. She loved to luxuriate in the presence of this man, and to feel - almost as a sunbather feels the sun - that warm male glow that came out of him to her when they were alone together. She loved him for the way he sat loosely in a chair, for the way he came in a door, or moved slowly across the room with long strides. She loved the intent, far look in his eyes when they rested on her, the funny shape of the mouth, and especially the way he remained silent about his tiredness, sitting still with himself until the whisky had taken some of it away.

a What kind of person do you think Mrs Maloney is?
b Do you think she is happily married? Why/why not?
c Describe her physical appearance.
d What is Mr Maloney's routine in the evening?
e What kind of job do you think he has?
f What kind of person do you imagine him to be?
g What words are used to describe the room the couple are in?
h What impression do you have of the room?

2 Find a word in the text that means:

a a table (usually with drawers) placed against a wall (para 1)
b to look quickly (para 3)
c two adjectives that mean 'calm' (para 3)
d to close noisily (para 4)
e to make a noise like a bell (para 6)
f satisfied (para 7)

3 Listen to the next part of the story and decide if the following statements are true or false, according to the text. If they are false, give the correct answer.

a Patrick is not very talkative this evening.
b Mary is a very attentive wife.
c She assumes he is annoyed about something.
d Patrick works in the police force.
e Patrick is nervous about something.

4 In groups, discuss what you think Patrick is going to tell her.

5 Read the next part of the text and then answer the questions below.

1 And he told her. It didn't take long, four or five minutes at most, and she sat very still through it all, watching him with a kind of dazed horror as he went further and further away from her with each word.

2 'So there it is,' he added. 'And I know it's kind of a bad time to be telling you, but there simply wasn't any other way. Of course I'll give you money and see you're looked after. But there needn't really be any fuss. I hope not anyway. It wouldn't be very good for my job.'

3 Her first instinct was not to believe any of it, to reject it all. It occurred to her that perhaps he hadn't even spoken, that she herself had imagined the whole thing. Maybe, if she went about her business and acted as though she hadn't been listening, then later, when she sort of woke up again, she might find none of it had ever happened.

4 'I'll get the supper,' she managed to whisper, and this time he didn't stop her.

a *And he told her.* What do you think he told her?
b What does he means by *it's a bad time to be telling you?*
c What does he mean by *there needn't really be any fuss?*
d What do you think will happen next?

LESSON 1   UNIT 1 MURDER!

6 The story now jumps to a later time (we have missed some out). Read the next part of the text and answer the questions.

> A few minutes later she got up and went to the phone. She knew the number of the police station, and when the man at the other end answered, she cried to him, 'Quick! Come quick! Patrick's dead!'
> 'Who's speaking?'
> 'Mrs Maloney. Mrs Patrick Maloney.'
> 'You mean Patrick Maloney's dead?'
> 'I think so,' she sobbed. 'He's lying on the floor and I think he's dead.'
> 'Be right over,' the man said.
> The car came very quickly, and when she opened the front door, two policemen walked in. She knew them both - she knew nearly all the men at that precinct - and she fell right into Jack Noonan's arms, weeping hysterically. He put her gently into a chair, then went over to join the other one, who was called O'Malley, kneeling by the body.
> 'Is he dead?' she cried.
> 'I'm afraid he is. What happened?'
> Briefly, she told her story about going to the grocer and coming back to find him on the floor. While she was talking, crying and talking, Noonan discovered a small patch of congealed blood on the dead man's head. He showed it to O'Malley who got up at once and hurried to the phone.

a   What is the matter with Patrick?
b   How does Mary feel? Which words tell you this?
c   How does Mary know the policemen?
d   What are their names?
e   What does Noonan find on the dead man's head?

In groups, predict how Patrick Maloney has died.

HOMEWORK

'I'll get the supper,' she managed to whisper, and this time he didn't stop her.

Write the missing part of the story which connects what Mary says to her husband (above) to when she phones the police (below):

A few minutes later she got up and went to the phone.

UNIT 1 MURDER!

2 'Don't make supper for me. I'm going out.'

1 Read out the stories you wrote for homework in groups and decide who has the best one.

2 Read the part of the story which was missed out earlier (continuing from when Patrick has told his wife the news). Using a dictionary to help you with any difficult vocabulary, decide if the statements opposite are true or false according to the text.

  a Mary felt shocked.
  b At this point she decided to murder her husband.
  c She hit him with a steel club.
  d She began to panic.
  e She was afraid of what would happen to her.

---

1 When she walked across the room she couldn't feel her feet touching the floor. She couldn't feel anything at all - except a slight nausea and a desire to vomit. Everything was automatic now - down the stairs to the cellar, the light switch, the deep freeze, the hand inside the cabinet taking hold of the first object it met. She lifted it out, and looked at it. It was wrapped in paper, so she took off the paper and looked at it again.

   A leg of lamb.

2 All right then, they would have lamb for supper. She carried it upstairs, holding the thin bone-end of it with both her hands, and as she went through the living-room, she saw him standing over by the window with his back to her, and she stopped.
   'For God's sake,' he said, hearing her, but not turning round.
   'Don't make supper for me. I'm going out.'

3 At that point, Mary Maloney simply walked up behind him and without any pause she swung the big frozen leg of lamb high in the air and brought it down as hard as she could on the back of his head.

   She might just as well have hit him with a steel club.

4 She stepped back a pace, waiting, and the funny thing was that he remained standing there for at least four or five seconds, gently swaying. Then he crashed to the carpet.
   The violence of the crash, the noise, the small table overturning, helped bring her out of the shock. She came out slowly, feeling cold and surprised, and she stood for a while blinking at the body, still holding the ridiculous piece of meat tight with both hands.

   All right, she told herself, so I've killed him.

5 It was extraordinary, now, how clear her mind became all of a sudden. She began thinking very fast. As the wife of a detective, she knew quite well what the penalty would be. That was fine. It made no difference to her. In fact, it would be a relief. On the other hand, what about the child? What were the laws about murderers with unborn children? Did they kill them both - mother and child? Or did they wait until the tenth month? What did they do?

6 Mary Maloney didn't know. And she certainly wasn't prepared to take a chance.

LESSON 2 **UNIT 1 MURDER!**

3 What do you think she will do next? Discuss in groups.

4 Try to remember the context in which the verbs below were used in the text. Put them into the past tense and make a sentence with each one.

Example *lift*
She lifted it (the meat) out of the freezer.

a wrap   b carry   c swing   d step
e sway   f crash   g blink

5 Listen to the next part of the story. In what order did Mary do the following things? Number them i-vii.

a went to her bedroom
b went shopping
c practised what she would say
d washed her hands
e put the meat in the oven
f put on some make-up
g got her coat
h spoke to Sam

6 Read the next part of the text and answer the questions which follow.

And now, she told herself as she hurried back, all she was doing now, she was returning home to her husband and he was waiting for his supper; and she must cook it good, and make it as tasty as possible because the poor man was tired; and if, when she entered the house, she happened to find anything unusual, or tragic, or terrible, then naturally it would be a shock and she'd become frantic with grief and horror. Mind you, she wasn't expecting to find anything. She was just going home with the vegetables. Mrs Patrick Maloney going home on a Thursday evening to cook supper for her husband.

That's the way, she told herself. Do everything right and natural. Keep things absolutely natural and there'll be no need for acting at all.

Therefore, when she entered the kitchen by the back door, she was humming a little tune to herself and smiling.

'Patrick!' she called. 'How are you, darling?'

She put the parcel down on the table and went through into the living-room; and, when she saw him lying there on the floor with his legs doubled up and one arm twisted back underneath his body, it really was rather a shock. All the old love and longing for him welled up inside her, and she ran over to him, knelt down beside him, and began to cry her heart out. It was easy. No acting was necessary.

Soon, other men began to come into the house. First a doctor, then two detectives, one of whom she knew by name. Later, a police photographer arrived and took pictures, and a man who knew about fingerprints. There was a great deal of whispering and muttering beside the corpse, and the detectives kept asking her a lot of questions. But they always treated her kindly.

UNIT 1 MURDER! **LESSON 2**

   a What does Mary tell herself on the way home?

   b How does she behave as she goes into the house?

   c How does she react when she sees her husband?

Mary phones the police and tells them what has happened.
(see Lesson 1)

7 Work in groups of three. One of you is Mary and two of you are the detectives. The detectives should ask Mary questions which she has to answer.

8 Fill in this Incident Report Form which the police had to complete.

HOMEWORK

Write the police report based on the notes above.

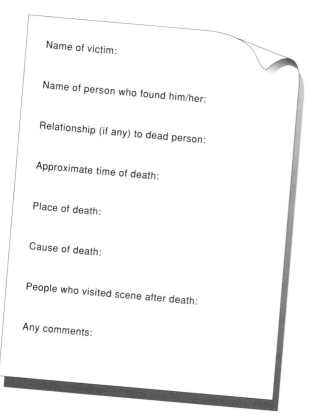

Name of victim:

Name of person who found him/her:

Relationship (if any) to dead person:

Approximate time of death:

Place of death:

Cause of death:

People who visited scene after death:

Any comments:

UNIT 1 MURDER!

3 'Get the weapon and you've got the man.'

1 In the next extract the detectives are interviewing Mary.

> She told her story again, this time right from the beginning, when Patrick had come in, and she was sewing, and he was tired, so tired he hadn't wanted to go out for supper. She told how she'd put the meat in the oven - 'it's there now, cooking' - and how she'd slipped out to the grocer for vegetables, and come back to find him lying on the floor.
> 'Which grocer?' one of the detectives asked. She told him, and he turned and whispered something to the other detective who immediately went outside into the street.

a What was her reason for going to the grocer's?
b What do you think the detective whispered to the other detective?

> In fifteen minutes he was back with a page of notes and there was more whispering, and through her sobbing she heard a few of the whispered phrases - '. . . acted quite normal . . . very cheerful . . . wanted to give him a good supper . . . peas . . . cheesecake . . . impossible that she . . .'

2 In pairs, act out the dialogue between Sam and the detective. Begin like this:

Detective: *I believe a Mrs Mary Maloney came to your shop this evening?*

3 Read the next part of the text and answer the questions below.

> After a while, the photographer and the doctor departed and two other men came in and took the corpse away on a stretcher. Then the fingerprint man went away. The two detectives remained, and so did the two policemen. They were exceptionally nice to her, and Jack Noonan asked if she wouldn't rather go somewhere else, to her sister's house perhaps, or to his own wife who would take care of her and put her up for the night.
>
> No, she said. She didn't feel she could move even a yard at the moment. Would they mind awfully if she stayed just where she was until she felt better? She didn't feel too good at the moment, she really didn't.
>
> Then hadn't she better lie down on the bed? Jack Noonan asked.
>
> No, she said, she'd like to stay right where she was in this chair. A little later perhaps, when she felt better, she would move.

a What is a word for 'dead body' and the thing a dead body is taken away on?
b What three things did Jack Noonan suggest to Mary? What do you think his exact words were?
c Find an expression which means 'to give somebody a bed'.
d Why do you think Mary wanted to stay at home?

4 Look at the next part of the text and decide if the statements below are true or false, according to the text. Use a dictionary to help you with any new vocabulary.

So they left her there while they went about their business, searching the house. Occasionally one of the detectives asked her another question. Sometimes Jack Noonan spoke to her gently as he passed by. Her husband, he told her, had been killed by a blow on the back of the head administered with a heavy blunt instrument, almost certainly a large piece of metal. They were looking for the weapon. The murderer may have taken it with him, but on the other hand he may've thrown it away or hidden it somewhere on the premises.

'It's the old story,' he said. 'Get the weapon, and you've got the man.'

Later, one of the detectives came up and sat beside her. Did she know, he asked, of anything in the house that could've been used as the weapon? Would she mind having a look around to see if anything was missing - a very big spanner, for example, or a heavy metal vase.

They didn't have any heavy metal vases, she said.

'Or a big spanner?'
She didn't think they had a big spanner. But there might be some things like that in the garage.

The search went on. She knew that there were other policemen in the garden all around the house. She could hear their footsteps on the gravel outside, and sometimes she saw the flash of a torch through a chink in the curtains. It began to get late, nearly nine she noticed by the clock on the mantel. The four men searching the rooms seemed to be growing weary, a trifle exasperated.

a The police were right about how Patrick was killed.
b They were looking for the instrument that killed him.
c They were sure the weapon had been taken away from the house.
d They looked outside as well.
e It was dark outside.

5 What are the names of the weapons below?

LESSON 3 — UNIT 1 MURDER!

6 Listen to the final part of the story and complete these sentences:

   a Mary persuades the policemen _____ .

   b Sergeant Noonan reminds her about _____ .

   c She asks the policemen to do her a favour by _____ .

   d They think the weapon is still _____ _____ .

   e Mary laughs because the policemen say it is probably _____ .

7 a What do you think happens to Mary in the end? Do you think she is found out?

   b Think of a title of the story.

8 a Read the whole story from beginning to end, including the listening tapescripts (at the back of the book).

   b Write down any new vocabulary you want to remember.

HOMEWORK

Write the newspaper report which came out the day after Patrick's death. Think of a headline.

UNIT 2 HEALTH AND FITNESS

4 You Are What You Eat

1 Match the pictures with each of the relevant categories below. An example is done for you.

prunes   biscuits   beans   cabbage

yoghurt   duck   sardines   pasta

sole   lamb   grapes

Dairy food		yoghurt
Fish	oily	
	white	
Meat	red	
	poultry	
Vegetables	green	
	pulse	
Fruit	fresh	
	dried	
Confectionery		
Cereals/bread, etc.		

Add at least three more examples to each category.

2 Discuss which of the food groups (in the table) you think you should try to eat more than once a day for a healthy diet. Why? What shouldn't you eat too much of? Why?

You may find the following vocabulary useful in your discussion.

| fat | protein | sugar |
| calories | carbohydrate | vitamins |

Example *I think you should eat a lot of fruit because it contains vitamins and fibre.*

3 a How many ways of cooking food can you think of? Complete the missing letters below. The first is done for you.

i	Cook in fat or oil.	FRY
ii	Cook over a fire (usually outside).	_ _ R _ E _ _ E
iii	Cook in very hot water.	B _ _ _
iv	Cook (eggs and fish) in gently boiling water or other liquid.	_ O _ C _
v	Cook in front of fire or in hot oven.	R _ _ S _
vi	Cook slowly and gently in closed pan.	_ T _ W
vii	Cook under direct heat.	G _ _ _ L
viii	Cook in a deep covered dish.	_ A _ _ E _ _ L _

b How do you normally prefer to cook/have cooked your:

meat   fish   eggs   vegetables

Compare with others in the class.

11

LESSON 4 — UNIT 2 HEALTH AND FITNESS

4 Do the quiz 'Test your diet to see how healthy it is'. Tick **a, b, c** or **d** depending what your eating habits are.

TEST YOUR DIET TO SEE HOW HEALTHY IT IS

1 How often do you eat a mixed salad (more than four vegetables), raw vegetables, or green leafy vegetables?
   a most days
   b 4-5 times a week
   c once or twice a week
   d seldom or never

2 How often do you eat a piece of fresh fruit?
   a once or more a day
   b three or four times a week
   c three or four times a month
   d seldom or never

3 Do you eat red meat or meat products:
   a at least once a day?
   b four or five times a week?
   c once or twice a week?
   d seldom or never?

4 How often do you eat three or four slices of wholemeal bread a day, or a main meal based on pulses: beans, lentils, etc?
   a four or more times a week
   b two or three times a week
   c two or three times a month
   d seldom or never

5 How often do you eat fish?
   a oily fish (salmon, trout, mackerel, herring, tuna) twice or more a week
   b oily and/or white fish and canned fish twice or more a week
   c fish and chips once a week, or more
   d seldom or never eat fish

6 What kind of breakfast do you eat?
   a none, or just tea or coffee
   b cereal with milk and sugar, or white toast and jam or marmalade
   c wholemeal toast with polyunsaturated or low-fat spread
   d whole grain cereal without added sugar and with low-fat milk

7 How many cake, biscuit or ice-cream snacks are there in your diet?
   a more than two a day
   b one a day
   c one or two a week
   d hardly any

8 How often do you eat fried food, or food roasted with added fat?
   a once or more a day
   b most days, or every other day
   c three or four times a week
   d once a week or less

5 Listen to a health expert giving the results of the quiz.

   a Listen once and find out how healthy your diet is. Make a note of what you get for each question.

   b Add up your score and compare it with other people.

   c Were you correct about which food you should eat a lot of and the reasons why? What should you personally eat more and less of according to the quiz?

6 Look at the interview with Julia Lawson, a lawyer.

   a In which paragraphs does she talk about:
      i   what she eats at different meals
      ii   what she likes drinking
      iii her weight
      iv   sweet food
      v   exercise

UNIT 2 HEALTH AND FITNESS — LESSON 4

1 'Well I don't seem to have any problems at all with putting on weight. I've been the same weight for the last ten years, I have lots of good intentions about taking exercise, but when it actually comes to it I often stay in bed instead or put my feet up in front of the television. I'm afraid I'm very lazy. Although I do take the dog out for a walk every day, so that's not too bad! And I go skiing once a year.

2 For breakfast I just have a cup of tea. I never have time for anything else so I'm starving by coffee time, and eat about eight biscuits! But at weekends I have a huge fried breakfast - eggs, bacon, tomatoes - the lot! At lunchtime I just have a snack - some soup, a salad, a sandwich, or something if I'm good, or a bar of chocolate if I'm not.

3 If either myself or my husband has the energy one of us might cook in the evenings. We like pasta, Indian curries, rice dishes and so on. But if we're too tired we just get some fish and chips from the shop, or a takeaway Chinese meal or something. We're very bad, and don't eat many vegetables or much fruit.

4 To drink I like mineral water, apple juice, coffee and tea. I also love red wine and gin and tonic.

5 My secret weakness is chocolate, which I adore. I have a sweet tooth for chocolate and chocolate puddings and I have to try not to eat too much.'

b What advice do you think the health expert would give Julia?
Work in pairs. One of you should imagine you are Julia. The other person should imagine you are the health expert. Ask Julia questions and give her advice.

7 a What five questions do you think the journalist asked Julia when he was doing the interview? Try to think of as many different ways of asking questions as you can.

Example *Do you like sweet food?*
Would you mind telling me if you like sweet food?

b Ask your partner the same questions. Make notes and then write up your notes as a text. Use the ones asked of Julia as an example.

8 Work out a series of questions so that you can interview people outside your class about their food and fitness routine. Use questions similar to the ones above, and any others you can think of.

Example *Could you tell me what you eat in a typical day?*
Do you take any exercise?

HOMEWORK

a   Ask two people to fill in the questionnaire.
b   Write up one of the questionnaires in the form of an interview. Use the interview with Julia as an example.

UNIT 2 HEALTH AND FITNESS

5 It'll Never Happen to Me!

BRITISH HEART FOUNDATION
Guide to a healthy heart

1 This illustration is taken from a leaflet which is trying to help to prevent heart disease.

a Put the vocabulary in the box into categories according to which of the three verbs below it is associated with.

Eat   Drink   Sleep

| munch   sip   gulp   devour   snooze |
| gobble   doze   knock back   nibble |
| nap   chomp |

b What do you think the person in the picture above should/shouldn't do if he wants to avoid a heart attack? Look carefully at the picture and make as many points as possible.

2 Compare your points with the ones below and think of a heading for each paragraph.

Example *Take regular exercise for paragraph 4.*

1   If you smoke your chances of getting heart disease are at least double those of a non-smoker. And the more you smoke, the greater the risk. And, if that isn't enough to make you stop, smoking also causes other serious diseases. It is expensive and makes your clothes and breath smell. The best advice is don't start or, if you do smoke, stop now.

2   One or two drinks a day won't do your heart any harm. But heavy drinking (more than two pints of beer or four glasses of wine a day) can lead to high blood pressure and strokes. You should also avoid binge drinking.

3   One in three British adults is overweight. The more overweight you are, the more likely you are to get high blood pressure or diabetes - both of which can lead to heart attacks and angina (heart pain). The best way to stay trim is to cut down on fatty and sugary foods and to take more exercise.

4   Regular exercise such as running, brisk walking, climbing stairs, swimming, cycling - even disco dancing - can help to protect your heart - and can be good fun too!
Whatever your age, it's never too late to start taking some form of regular exercise. Choose an activity you really enjoy and try to set aside two or three hours a week to spend on it. If you think you are very unfit, consult your doctor before starting.

5   Your everyday choice of food - especially the amount of fat in your food - is important to the health of your heart. If you love your heart you should eat less fatty foods such as meat, dairy products, cakes and biscuits and more poultry, fish, vegetables, fruit and salads. Switch to polyunsaturated margarine and oils.

UNIT 2 HEALTH AND FITNESS — LESSON 5

3 Find words or expressions in the text that are more or less the opposite of the following. The first letter of each word or expression is given

a half (para 1)   d _____

b moderate (para 2)   h _____

c regular and moderate (para 2)   b _____

d fat (para 3)   t _____

e slow (para 4)   b _____

f keep the same (para 5)   s _____

4 Listen to an extract from a radio interview where a doctor gives advice on how to avoid heart problems and answer the following questions:

a What are the 'six golden rules'?
b How can you avoid high blood pressure?
c Why can stress cause heart attacks?
d How can you avoid stress?
e Why is exercise good for you?
f What are the suggestions for improving your diet?

5 a Read the letter opposite and find out:

i What is the relationship between the writer of the letter and the receiver?
ii What is her main bit of news?
iii What other reason(s) does she have for writing?

b Discuss what advice you can give Marie to help her husband avoid another heart attack. Use the information you have read about and listened to in this unit.

14, Linton Park,
Oxford
OX2 3AS

11th August

Dear Sarah,

Thanks very much for your letter, which I've been meaning to reply to for ages. I'm afraid life has been very busy here and I've also had rather a shock recently as James has been in hospital with a minor heart attack. He's out of hospital now and seems much better, but obviously the worry about it happening again is always on my mind.

As you know, he's nearly 50 now and I suppose most people begin to put on weight at around that age. But one of the main problems is that he has to go out for all these heavy business lunches and then sitting down at a desk all day can't really help! And with all the stress of his new job he's smoking much too much, as well. I'm sure all this must have helped to cause this heart attack.

I'm trying to make sure he gets as much rest as possible, almost forcing him to sit down in front of the television when he gets home, but I worry a lot about if he's eating the right things and so on. The doctor hasn't really been much help!

Anyway, enough of our problems! Why don't you come and stay with us one weekend when you have time? We've got plenty of space now that Nicola has left home and James would love to see you. We hardly ever see our friends these days.

I hope you're well and that you enjoyed your holiday.
See you soon,
Love,

Marie

HOMEWORK

Write the letter which Marie sent to Sarah. Give suggestions on things such as diet, exercise and smoking. Accept her invitation to stay, and suggest a date. Ask if you can bring someone with you.

UNIT 2 — HEALTH AND FITNESS

Confessions of Food and Drink Junkies

1 Look at the two newspaper headlines below. What do you think the texts are going to be about?

I'M ADDICTED TO COKE
Docs called in to cure cola-holic

Text 1

2 Read both texts quickly and answer the questions:

HOOKED ON NICOTINE

Text 2

SOFT DRINK addict Chris Maynard knocks back 40 cans of Coca-Cola every day.

The jobless 30 year old has resorted to selling the furniture from his home in New Milton, Hampshire to pay for his £70 a week habit.

Chris, whose plight came to light when he appeared in court at Totton accused of motoring offences, is about to be treated by specialists at Guy's Hospital, London.

Doctors say he is slowly being poisoned by a massive overdose of caffeine. He said yesterday: 'I get the shakes, I am always hungry and I can't sleep". Chris - who lives on £26 a week social security - spends up to £70 a week on the drink to keep his fridge full and can't make it through the day without gallons of Coke.

He said: 'I started by selling the carpet to get money for Coke and now all I have left is my dog Ben and a computer'.

A spokesman for the American soft drinks firm said he had never heard of anyone drinking up to 40 cans a day. He said: 'There are no harmful ingredients in Coke but any product taken to excess - even water - could cause problems".

The perils of smoking came tragically early for one man. Dave, as he will be known, started smoking as early as twelve, a move which has scarred his life ever since.

The pressure to take up smoking from his friends grew so intense, like a powerful magnet, he felt helpless to resist the urge. The threat of social abandonment at a time when smoking was high on the list of fashionable things to do was the biggest reason for starting smoking.

He tried to hide his secret from his mother, who he knew would be deeply upset.

Nicotine

He used feeble excuses at the local newsagent in order to get his daily fix of nicotine. Unfortunately for him his newsagent was trusting and believed him when he said they were for someone else. Dave deeply wanted to give up and still wants to up to this very day. 'At one stage I managed to give up for two weeks, but I started shaking and sweating'. He added that he was a different man when he stopped smoking, becoming angry, tensed up and unreasonable. 'I would dearly love to stop now but I can't,' he sighed.

UNIT 2 HEALTH AND FITNESS — LESSON 6

a How many cans of Coke does Chris drink a day?
b How much does it cost him a week?
c How was his problem discovered?
d What are the physical symptoms of the addiction?
e How much money does he have a week?
f When did 'Dave' start smoking?
g Why did he start?
h What did his mother say?
i How did he manage to get cigarettes when he was young?
j What happened when he tried to give up?

3 Look at the texts again, more closely.

Text 1
Find a word or expression similar to:

a he drinks
b turned to (for help)
c serious situation
d was discovered
e too much (of a drug)

Text 2
How can you say the following expressions in another way?

f has scarred his life ever since
g the pressure to take up smoking from his friends grew so intense
h the threat of social abandonment
i his daily fix of nicotine

4 Discuss the following questions in groups:

a What do you think might have caused Chris' addiction?
b What other food and drink addictions do you know of?
c What are the physical symptoms of these addictions?
d Do you think Chris or Dave will ever be able to give up? How many ways do you know to get over such addictions?
e Is smoking a problem in your country? Is it encouraged or discouraged?
f Are there any laws to prevent people from smoking in certain places or under certain ages?

5 In pairs one of you (Student A) should take the role of Chris and the other (Student B) of the journalist. The journalist should ask Chris questions. Base your interview on the article but add any extra details you want. Student A should then be the journalist and Student B should be Dave.

6 Do a survey of the people in your class to find out how many students have addictions. Report back in groups.

7 Listen to Gillie talking about her addictions and complete the following information according to the text.

a She was addicted to _____ and _____ .
b If she didn't get her 'fix' she would feel _____ and if she saw someone eating chocolate she'd feel like _____ .
c She noticed her coffee was getting _____ and _____ and as a result she wasn't _____ .
d Eventually she realised how _____ she was becoming, so she went to see an _____ who had been _____ to her.
e This woman advised her to _____ .
f She spent _____ to get that advice.

HOMEWORK

Interview at least two people about their addictions and write a short report on each of them based on the newspaper reports earlier in the lesson.

UNIT 3   EARNING A LIVING

7   The Job or the Money?

1 a What are the jobs above? Which do you think would:

be the hardest work?
be the most exciting?
be the most satisfying?
be the best paid?
require the longest training?
be the most (socially) useful?
be the most stressful?

b Work in groups. Each of you should choose one of the people in the pictures and describe what you think he/she does in a typical day. The other people in the group must guess which job you are describing.

Example *He or she has to plan what to put in the garden and choose what plants and/or vegetables to grow.*

c Which do you think would be the advantages and disadvantages of each job?

2 a Listen to Pam and Hag talking about their jobs and match the speakers to the jobs in the pictures in **1**.

b Write down what they like and dislike about their jobs

c Explain what Pam meant by:

i licensing hours
ii anti-social hours
iii shifts
iv the 'bar bore'

3 a A journalist interviewed a nurse called Penny Sharman about her job. Before you read the interview, do the following vocabulary exercise.

i What is the name of a person who is ill?
p _____ .
ii What is the name of a 'room' in a hospital where these people sleep?
w _____ .
iii A period of time that you have to work. Nurses sometimes work day and sometimes night ones.
s _____ .

b Write down as many other words as possible connected to hospitals or nursing and compare what you have written in groups.

4 a The journalist asked Penny Sharman the following questions, but the text got jumbled up. In what order do the paragraphs go? This is the order in which the questions were asked.

i What made you decide to be a nurse?
ii What was the training like?
iii What kind of wards do you work on?
iv What hours do you work?
v Where do you live?
vi What do you do in a normal day?
vii What do you like about your job?

UNIT 3 EARNING A LIVING — LESSON 7

1 'We do have good fun in the nurse's home, though it's like a boarding school with no rules. My little room here costs around £45 a month, which is deducted from my salary. I end up with about £220 a month so I could never afford to rent in Brighton where it's £30 weekly upwards for shared housing. I do get fed up with the lack of privacy, sharing a kitchen and bathroom, but at least it's warm.

2 'We get eight or nine week allocations on all the different wards. So far I've been on General Medical, Geriatrics, Paediatrics (children's ward) - that was my favourite - Orthopaedics, Surgical and Theatre.

3 'A typical day on the wards? I arrive at 7.45am and listen to reports from the night staff. I will be allocated between three and seven patients for whom I have total care. I'll start by helping them wash, then serve and clear away breakfast. Next I take their temperatures, pulses and blood pressure. Perhaps some patients will need help with getting out of bed and walking around. Then it's around lunchtime. In between there's always plenty of bedpans to sort out and beds to tidy. I like to spend a lot of time with patients, talking and reassuring, which I feel is an essential part of nursing. But there isn't always enough time, we're so busy doing other things. Nurses shouldn't really do domestic jobs like serving meals but we do.

4 Nursing is something I've always wanted to do. I left school at 16 with seven 'O' levels and did a pre-nursing course, which I haven't found that helpful. I chose Brighton because it was fairly near my home town of Guildford. Plus I knew it was a lively place and I'd heard the nursing school was good.

5 'Nursing is tough but I do enjoy my job. Nothing can beat seeing a very ill patient make a complete recovery. Job satisfaction is very high. I have a varied life and meet all kinds of different people. Nursing is a good route into other things as well. For instance I could use my RGN qualifications to get into university, perhaps to do Social Psychology. Then I might go back into nursing, as a community nurse - an area I'm very interested in.

6 'Training is very practically orientated. Once we'd done six weeks in the classrooms at the Brighton School of Nursing it was straight out into the wards - very scary! We're called 'student' nurses but I don't feel there's much time for 'studying' - we just get right on with nursing.

7 'I work shifts. An 'early' is from 7.45am to 4.30pm and a 'late' is 12.30 in the afternoon to 9.30pm. I work nights sometimes, too. We should get one weekend off in three but it's not always possible. The trouble is that you don't know if you're off duty until shortly before so it can be difficult to make arrangements. My work definitely interferes with my social life.

b Are the following statements about Penny's interview true or false?

i Most of the training is theoretical.
ii The nurse's home is very strict.
iii Nurses don't have enough time to talk to patients.
iv There are a lot of opportunities in this job.

5 a What jobs can you think of which are 'socially necessary and useful' but which are badly paid and hard work? Are they mainly done by men or women?

b Which jobs are paid well? Why? Are they mainly done by men or women?

6 Paul works in a very stressful and demanding job in the City of London (the financial centre of London).

a Why do you think he does this kind of work, and what do you think the problems are?

 b Listen to Paul talking about his job and answer the following questions:

i What does he do in his job?
ii What does he find stressful about working in London?
iii What is the atmosphere like in the dealing room?
iv What signs are there that people are stressed?
v How long can people work in this kind of job?

c What other jobs are as stressful and demanding as Paul's?

HOMEWORK

Talk to somebody about the work they do, and their daily routine. Ask them what the good and bad things are about their job and write it up as a short article. Use the article about nursing as a model.

UNIT 3   EARNING A LIVING

8 Jobs with a Difference

Professor Gresham is a forensic pathologist. A pathologist is a doctor who examines dead people to find out how they died. A forensic pathologist uses his scientific knowledge to help the police to find criminals.

1 a Think of any questions you would like to ask the Professor if you were interviewing him. Discuss these questions.

  b Listen to the Professor to see if your questions were answered.

  c Listen to the Professor again and complete the information below.

  i When somebody is found dead the 'scenes of crime squad' are called. Tick which of the following they have to do (according to the Professor).

  take photographs   wall off the area
  take fingerprints   look for clues
  police the area

  ii The forensic pathologist usually arrives _____ later.
  iii His job is to:
  take the body temperature
  establish the _____ of death
  tell the police which _____ was used.
  iv What do the police need to know most urgently? Why?
  v Why is it so important to establish exactly how somebody died?
  vi What does the Professor find very difficult about his job?

2 a What kind of person do you think you would need to be to have a job like this? (For example - somebody with a strong stomach!)
  b Would you like to do this kind of job? Why/why not?

3 a The job of a holiday representative might seem glamorous to some people. Think of some reasons why.

  b Read the text and write down:

  i The two main things Cathy has to do when she goes abroad.
  ii The good things about her job.
  iii The bad things about it.

THE HOLIDAY REPRESENTATIVE

THIS YEAR CATHY BARTROP has been to Australia, Thailand, Hong Kong, Singapore and the Seychelles, staying in five star hotels and sampling the local cuisine.

Not surprising, then, that Cathy looks tanned and healthy. But that, she says, is thanks to a holiday in Majorca, not her jet-setting job. As business development manager for travel firm Thomas Cook, Cathy, 27, has one of the best perks imaginable: all-expenses-paid trips to the most exotic corners of the world.

Yet she insists that her job is far from being one long holiday. 'It annoys me when people say what a wonderful job I must have. They perceive it as very glamorous, but in fact it's very hard work. I'm usually in the country for only a short time, and there's a lot to pack in.'

Before a new resort is included in the Thomas Cook brochure, Cathy and her colleagues have to go and check it out, see if there are adequate facilities, and that it offers good value to tourists.

She also takes groups of travel agents abroad and shows them around, allowing then to see the places for themselves and then - it is hoped - sell them to the customer.

'When I go somewhere I have to know what all the selling points are for the various locations, so I take the same tours as the tourists and visit all the local attractions,' says Cathy.

The worst aspect of her work is the jet-lag that comes from long-haul travel. 'And staying alone in hotels can be difficult as well, though I've had more problems in the UK than abroad,' says Cathy. 'The hotels we use are all good ones which are used to business travellers, so you don't feel awkward.' Although she's been in the job for several years, Cathy still finds travel exciting, and looks forward to going abroad. 'I'm a bit of a freak - I even like being in airports!' she admits.

c What qualities would you need to have for a job like this? Think of at least four (for example, you would need to be independent).

4 Match the jobs in the list to the categories below. Use your dictionary to help you.

estate agent   journalist   newsreader   travel agent   actor   hairdresser   psychoanalyst   social worker   accountant   bank clerk   dancer   sales representative   air hostess   model

the media   travel   beauty or fashion   counselling   finance   mathematics   technology   the arts   selling

5 a Write down the adjectives below which you think describe you and discuss what you have written with someone else.

sociable   clever   independent   healthy   adventurous   patient   energetic   determined   a sense of humour   ambitious   flexible   practical/sensible   curious   efficient   gentle   sensitive

b Write down the three jobs you would most like to do. Write down five adjectives for each job and compare with someone else who chose the same job. Discuss your reasons.

6 a Look at the pictures below and match your palm to the picture which fits best. Read the text which goes with it.
b Does your palm reflect the sort of job you want to do?
c Do the qualities required for these jobs correspond with the ones you chose?

IT'S IN THE PALM OF YOUR HAND

EARTH HANDS
A short palm with stubby fingers. Earth hands belongs to a practical, level-headed, hard-working person. Of the four types they're the most determined, even 'plodding', in their approach to work. They enjoy being providers, so catering, cookery or anything to do with housing attracts them. They like to be close to the earth, so horticulture or farming are options.

AIR HANDS
A square-ish palm with a gentle rounding to it, with longer fingers than an Earth type. These people can't stick to routines. They're curious, 'buzzy', nosey types. Jobs which involve languages, talking to people, asking questions would appeal. Air types are happiest in the media, whether it's the press, television or films, or the travel industry.

FIRE HANDS
An oblong palm with short fingers. These people are fired by life. They're enthusiastic and physically active. They're good in sports jobs, and their impulsive and enthusiastic nature means they make good leaders and bosses. They're often extroverts who don't mind sticking their necks out or making a fool of themselves. Acting, music or teaching suit them.

WATER HANDS
A long, lean palm with long, fine fingers. They are gentle, sensitive and easily influenced! They are rarely leaders. The art world is full of Water-handed people. Many are drawn to the beauty, design or fashion business, from hairdressing to modelling to beauty therapy. Their sensitivity means they make excellent counsellors or therapists.

HOMEWORK

1 Ask two people to tell you what jobs they would most like to do (from the list in **4.**).
2 Look at their palm and see if it corresponds to what they want.
3 Do you think the description of their personality is accurate?

UNIT 3 EARNING A LIVING

9 A Job or Family Life?

The women interviewed are all from the same family. The oldest is 95 and a great-grandmother. She used to be a servant. The grandmother is 72, and the great grand-daughter, at 20, is a draughtsperson.

1 Discuss the likely differences in the lives of 95 year old Rose and 20 year old Catherine. Think about:

their schooldays
attitude to marriage
work

2 Form groups of three. Each person should read one of the following extracts and make notes using these headings:

a Name
b Age
c When did she leave school?
d What jobs did she do?
e Information on hours/salary?
f When did she stop work?
g What is/was her attitude to staying at home?
h Does she believe in equality?
i What does she think of working mothers?

3 Compare your notes in your groups. Tell each other about the woman you read about.

4 Discuss the following points:
a Did you get any surprises?
b Which women are similar to each other?
c What do the other two women think of Catherine's life?

GREAT-GRANDMA ROSE, 95

When I left school at 13 I went into service at a farmhouse. I was the only servant and I did everything. I'd get up at dawn and if the sun was shining, I'd work in the hayfields. If it rained I could stay in bed for an extra hour or two, then I'd do the housework. I'd clean all the silver, scrub the floors, and wash up. If I was in the house I'd wear a uniform - white apron and cap - but I didn't mind. I quite liked it, it was better than doing lessons in school.
I worked there for six months and earned £1 a month. I had lots of jobs - cook, cleaner, housekeeper - but I could pick and choose but the money was bad. I met my husband in a pub when I was working as a barmaid and as soon as we were married I gave up my job. We had a family straight away and I didn't miss working at all. But then my husband died and left me with three children so I had no alternative but to get a job. I was employed as housekeeper to a doctor and his wife and they always treated me as an equal. I stayed with them for 24 years. And I didn't retire until I was 74.
I wish I'd had the same chances as my great-granddaughter, Cathy is a lady of pleasure and leisure. I know she works hard but she'd work a damn sight harder if she had to do the house-work. I'd love to do her job.
But I do think there are too many women going out to work and leaving babies with childminders. I say, if you want a baby, stay at home and look after it.
It's good that women can choose what they want to do nowadays but there are some jobs which they shouldn't do. I think the Prime Minister should be a man - ruling the country is a man's job.

GRANDMOTHER GLADYS, 72

Dad died when I was five. I left school at 14 and got a job, as we needed the money. For 12 months I was a milkmaid and earned five shillings a week.
But then my auntie got me another job because she didn't think 'going out with the milk' was the right job for a young girl. For six years I worked in a tobacconist's shop six days a week, from 8.30a.m to 9 pm.
I met my husband in a coffee shop and I was glad to give up working. As my husband was a good provider I had more clothes and luxuries than I'd ever had.
I was never bored. After the housework was done I'd go and see my mum and it wasn't long before I became pregnant with my only daughter, Maureen. A lot of married women did go back to work to help with the war effort but I couldn't because of the baby. Mothers who go out to work miss all the pleasure of bring up their babies.
If you're clever, it's a shame to give up work, but women who think careers are more important shouldn't get married. My husband and I encouraged Maureen to

have a career but we left her to make her own decisions. There are marvellous opportunities open to women today and I'm terribly proud of my granddaughter. Cathy has taken after my mum - she's always been a fighter, but I prefer to be taken care of. The man should be the head of the household. I relied on my husband for everything. Now it seems strange that women are equal to men. I'm not sure if that's right.

DAUGHTER CATHERINE, 20

I'm a draughtsperson at Vickers, doing the same job my dad once did and I don't think I'm unusual. I'm just taking advantage of all the opportunities available. At school I enjoyed science subjects, and after talking it over with my parents and teachers, decided to concentrate on physics, maths and technical drawing. I passed my exams and after several interviews I started training at Vickers.

Mum nearly died the first day. To begin with I was doing manual work on the shop floor, and I walked out of the house in overalls and hobnail boots. The day started at 7.30a.m. and I'd come home flaked out - but compared to my great-gran I know I had it easy.

I've got my career planned - I hope to go to university to study computer-aided engineering and then I'll return to Vickers either as a design engineer or as a manager. I've never really had any doubts about what I wanted to do. I really do believe that there's no reason why a woman can't tackle any job - they can go on oil rigs and down mines, if they have the physical strength.

If I get married I've every intention of continuing with my career; that will always come first. People can be employed to clean the house if necessary. And I don't see why it should be women's work. Why can't the men iron shirts and cook and clean? Those jobs bore me rigid - I'm sure I'd go mad if I had to stay at home for very long.

I'd like to have a family eventually and I'd have absolutely no qualms about leaving a baby in someone else's care. But I'd probably wait until the child was three or four before I returned to work. I know my mum doesn't agree but I do think there's time for being with the family at weekends and evenings - you don't need to be there all the time.

Women are no longer second-class citizens. Men are beginning to sit up and think, they see women doing their jobs and they realise they're no better than us. Margaret Thatcher is an example to us all.

There's still some resentment, especially in my line of work, that I'm taking a man's job. They say, you'll be leaving to have kids in the next few years so why should you deprive a man of a job? I just say, what gives the man the right to say this is a man's job?

I'd encourage any daughter of mine to exercise her free choice. If she wants a career I'd back her all the way. The one thing I would make her realise is that if you study and get good qualifications it's a means to a better life.

5 Discuss the following questions.

a How is a man who stays at home to look after children regarded in your country?
b Would you like to do this/have a partner who does this? Why/why not?
c Do you think young children are better looked after by the mother, or do you think it is a job either partner can or should do?
d What problems do you think there might be?

6 Listen to this conversation between two men, one of whom (Tony) stayed at home to look after his baby son, Benjamin, while his wife went out to work.
Before listening, discuss what questions you would like to ask him.

a Listen and see if any of your questions were answered.

b Are the following statements true or false? Listen again to check your answers.
i Tony manages to combine writing with bringing up the child.
ii He finds Benjamin takes up a lot of time.
iii His wife would prefer to stay at home with the child.
iv Tony has had to have help in the house.
v His friends think it's very strange that Tony doesn't have a 'real job'.

7 In groups prepare a list of questions that you would like to ask a young couple and an older couple about their views on work and marriage and the bringing up of children.

Homework

Interview two couples of different ages, using the questions you wrote in class. Make notes so that you can report back to the class later.

UNIT 4 THE UNEXPLAINED

10 The Paranormal

1 Read the following story and answer the questions.

ANOTHER TIME, ANOTHER PLACE

When Nuala Walshe was introduced to Des, a tall handsome Australian who was visiting her remote village in the west of Ireland, she was delighted to meet the newcomer and their friendship swiftly blossomed into a closer relationship. Nuala, who had been brought up by an aunt after her mother died, was excitedly looking forward to her engagement day.

'On the day, Des had been invited by my aunt to have tea. I produced a letter of congratulations from my father who was living in England. I got the shock of my life when Des snatched the letter out of my hand and, in a fearful rage, tore it to pieces.

'Suddenly the room grew cold and I felt a strange cold draught. As I looked over at Des, I became terrified, because standing behind his chair was the figure of a dark-haired young man watching me with concern. I froze with fear and in an instant the man disappeared.

'Des had gone deathly white. He was staring into space as if he were looking at something behind my chair. Suddenly he passed out and collapsed on the floor.

'When he'd recovered, he said that a woman had appeared behind my chair. I didn't dare tell him what I had seen. When my aunt showed Des an old photograph of my mother, he told us it was the same woman.

'Des left on his own and as he walked to the gate he became aware of the cold atmosphere again, even though it was a beautiful warm August day. He stared in horror as he saw the bolt in the gate opening for him, as if bidding him to leave.

'As he drove away from the cottage, a woman loomed up in front of the car. He panicked as he recognised my dead mother. She was pointing to the distance, as if telling him to go away.

'When he arrived home and got out of the car, to his great relief the woman was nowhere to be be seen.

'The next day Des told me the engagement was off because he was certain my mother was trying to frighten him away.

'To get over the disappointment, I decided to visit my father and his new wife, Betty, in England. When there was a ring on the doorbell, Betty said it was probably her nephew, Jim.

'I couldn't believe my eyes when Jim entered the room. He was the man I had seen standing behind Des in my aunt's cottage. I was even more amazed when he smiled and said, 'Haven't we met before some place?'

a What did Nuala see behind Des's chair?
b What did Des see behind Nuala's chair?
c Who was it?
d What happened as he was driving away?
e Who was Jim?
f What do you think happens next?
g Write down all the expressions connected to fear and surprise.

2 This is the first line and the last line of another ghost story. The title is *The Dress*. In groups, guess what happens.

This story is about a bloke who was driving home one night late at night ... They opened the wardrobe and in the wardrobe they found this white dress, soaking wet.

3 a Listen to the story. How different was it to yours?
b Who was the little girl and why do you think she appeared to the speaker?

4 a How do you feel about ghost stories like this? Do you feel; afraid/sceptical/amused?
b Do you know any good ghost stories or have you seen any good ghost films? Tell each other the story and how you felt about it.

5 The following vocabulary is connected to the paranormal. Match the expressions to the definitions below.

a spontaneous combustion
b levitation
c clairvoyancy

i when somebody or something rises into the air, because of spiritualist powers
ii burning, (usually unexplained) caused by chemical changes
iii being able to see things (in the future) by a special power

UNIT 4 THE UNEXPLAINED · LESSON 10

6 a Match each of the paranormal beliefs above to one of the extracts below.

1 One night in December 1868 three gentlemen of 'unimpeachable reputation' sat together in the dark in an apartment on the upper floor of Ashley House in London. One of them was Lord Lindsay, a notable scientist, the second was Lord Adare, and the third his cousin, Captain Charles Wynne. All three were silent, nervous and tense as though waiting for something extraordinary to happen. After a few minutes they heard the window in the next room being raised and almost immediately saw the figure of Daniel Dunglas Home floating in the air outside the window of the room in which they were sitting. He must have been at least eighty feet from the ground. Lord Lindsay wrote later: 'The moon was shining full into the room... I saw Home's feet about six inches above the window sill. He remained in this position for a few seconds then raised the window, glided into the room feet foremost and sat down.' And Lord Adare gave his word: 'The fact of his having gone out of one window and in at the other, I can swear to.'

Although in his mature years Home could levitate at will and became best known to the general public for his spectacular drifting about in the air, he also levitated without seemingly being aware of it. On one occasion when his host drew his attention to the fact that he was hovering above the cushion in his armchair, Home seemed most surprised. To the end of his life he maintained that he could only fly through the air because he was lifted up by the spirits. 'Since the first time, I have never felt fear,' he wrote in his autobiography, 'Should I, however, have fallen from the ceiling of some rooms in which I have been raised, I could not have escaped serious injury. I am generally lifted up perpendicularly; my arms frequently become rigid and are drawn above my head as if I were grasping the unseen power which slowly raises me from the floor...'

---

2 A year before the outbreak of the Second World War, Mrs Mary Carpenter, on a boating holiday in East Anglia, burst into flames and was reduced to ashes in front of her horrified husband and children. There was no flame from which she could have caught fire.

---

3 Christine Ross has been 'receiving' messages since the age of ten. She 'saw' the man she was to marry and the pub they would live in. She also experiences visions: 'I have tried to switch off but it doesn't work. These days I try to 'go with it'. People say it is a gift but it can only be that if I can learn how to use it. The most recent occasion was when a little boy went missing from Butlin's at Ayr. I saw a picture of him lying in a ditch at the bottom of a steep grassy slope. There was a hill nearby with trees at the top. I rang the police incident room and told them. Then on the Sunday afternoon I told a friend that I felt the boy had been found. The next day it was in the paper; he was found in the Carrick hills and the photograph was the 'picture' I had received'.

b Look through all the texts again quickly and try to answer the following questions. Work in pairs and try to work out the meaning of any vocabulary you don't know.

i Could Dunglas Home levitate when he wanted to?
ii How did he do it, according to him?
iii Where was Mrs Carpenter when she burst into flames?
iv What 'picture' did Christine Ross receive?

c Do you know any similar stories? Tell each other stories you know, in groups.

7 Invent a ghost story based on the pictures below.

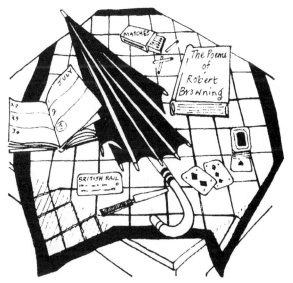

a Work individually and think up a possible context.
b Discuss your story in pairs.
c Write a story in groups of six. Work in pairs, with each pair beginning the story and passing it round for the next pair to continue.
d Decide which of the three stories are the best.

HOMEWORK

Write a ghost story. Either write the one above, or another one you know if you prefer.

UNIT 4 — THE UNEXPLAINED

11 Out of Body Experiences

1 Some people have suffered strange experiences, when they feel that they have been taken out of their body. Some experiences are more dramatic and are better termed 'Near Death Experiences'. The experiences are not necessarily bad but are often connected with illness and can leave a strong effect on the person concerned.

2 This is a painting of heaven done by someone who suffered a 'Near Death Experience'. What does this show about life after death? Do you agree that it might be like this?

Which of these words, if any, do you associate with death? Add any others you can think of.

terror   peace   detachment   darkness
light   joy   music   white   blue   black
tunnel   mist   float   despair   pain   relief

3 Listen to a phone-in on the radio with people who have had a 'Near Death Experience'.

a Listen to each of the three extracts, and complete the sentences below.

TOM
i Tom fell into the sea because _____ .
ii He saw _____ before he 'came back'.
iii Afterwards, in hospital, he felt _____ .

SUSAN
iv Susan was in hospital _____ when things started to go wrong.
v She saw _____ and felt _____ .
vi She wanted to return because _____ .

JANE
vii Jane floated _____ .
viii She heard _____ and saw _____ .
ix She was told _____ and returned to hospital.

b Do these extracts confirm your views of what death might be like?

c Which of the words in 2 above do they use when describing their experiences?

4 a There are six stages associated with 'Near Death Experiences'. From what you heard before, what order do you think they come in?

i Entering the darkness which leads to light.
ii Arrival at 'heaven'.
iii A change of personality.
iv The 'out of the body' experience.
v The return.
vi An altered state - a feeling of peace.

b Read the texts and put them in order.

c Match the paragraph to the relevant heading in **4a**.

1 Then they regain consciousness - it is a feeling which has been described as being pulled back like a piece of elastic. They start to feel pain again, and also feel very distressed about having returned.

2 Then there is usually a strange buzzing noise in the ears and a feeling as if the soul has escaped from the body. In some cases it is attached to the top of the head at first, by a silvery cord, but that eventually floats away. People who have NDEs at this point sometimes hover near the ceiling and often feel that it is a bit silly or boring. Or they sometimes float about the hospital, eavesdropping on people's conversations, which can be useful evidence later.

3 People often change quite a lot as a result of it. They are less worried about the material aspects of life and more interested in the spiritual, although some people who have previously been very religious might not be interested in their religion any more. Nobody who has suffered an NDE ever fears death again and many of them are fascinated by the paranormal.

4 Most people describe it as a garden full of a magical light and (usually blue) colour. At times wonderful music can be heard. The NDErs look around the place and meet relatives and friends who have died. These deceased relatives and friends often tell them things about the future which often come true. But the experiences ends here, with the NDErs being told they have to return and finish their time on earth.

5 Next is the feeling of being pulled very fast up a dark tunnel with a bright light at the end. Some people see a bright figure at the end. One would expect them to be afraid, but people say they felt incredibly excited and happy, and had warm feelings. Some NDErs are told to go back at this stage because they are not ready to die. However, most people beg to be allowed to stay and if they do they arrive at their destination.

6 If they are about to die it is either because a person is critically ill or has been in a serious accident and therefore they are usually in great pain or suffering great terror, which is not helped by the distress of the relatives of this person. Suddenly, however, there is a feeling of peace and great happiness.

d What is said in these texts which is not mentioned by the people who phoned in?

HOMEWORK

Write an imaginary letter to Steve Redmond, the producer of the radio programme, telling him about your 'Out of the Body' or 'Near Death' Experiences.

UNIT 4 — THE UNEXPLAINED

12 Debating the Issue

You are going to take part in a panel discussion entitled 'Near Death Experiences - fact or fiction?'

Work in groups. One group (Group A) is going to defend the motion and the other group (Group B) is going to attack it.

Preparation for the Debate

1
  a Write down a list of points either for or against the idea of Near Death Experiences. Use the suggested 'ideas to help you.

  b Try to anticipate the arguments the other group are going to come up with, and think of an answer to them.

  c Think of as many ways of giving opinions and agreeing and disagreeing as you can. Look at the Useful Language. Which expressions do you think are the most and least strong? Practise saying them with suitable intonation.

  d Include in your arguments evidence from a 'real life witness' -one of your group can pretend to have had an NDE.

GROUP A: Ideas

- Listen to the tape in Lesson 11 again, (or read the tapescript at the back of the book), and look again at the reading text. Both are in lesson 11 in this unit.
- Make a list of all the reasons you can think of as to why the experiences should be taken seriously.
- Decide in what order you should make the points.
- Have a 'real life witness' to give his/her experience as convincingly as possible.
- Think of questions which you will ask the other group, or points you will make, to try to defeat their argument.
- Appoint two 'spokespeople' to present the case, as well as the 'witness/witnesses'.

GROUP B: Ideas

- Think of as many reasons as you can why these experiences cannot really be valid and try to suggest other explanations for them. Make a list of these reasons.

Example The out of body sensation is really a trick of the mind and really the floating is based on memory and imagination.
The dark tunnels are the visual cells which are not working well, as people are dying. It could be due to lack of oxygen.

- One of you should invent a 'negative' experience that you had, which you think disproves

UNIT 4 THE UNEXPLAINED — LESSON 12

the other experiences you heard or read about above. Argue for it being the effect of drugs, etc. when you are very ill.

- Decide in what order you will make the points.

- Think of questions to ask the other group, or points to put to them, which may defeat their argument.

- Decide on two 'spokespeople' from your group as well as a 'witness' who will present your case.

Useful Language

Giving opinions
In my opinion . . .
I think/believe . . .
It is clear/obvious that . . .
There is no doubt that . . .
Don't you think that . . . ?

Agreeing
Exactly!
I couldn't agree more.
(I agree) absolutely.
That's true.
You've got a point, but . . .
Possibly, but . . .

Disagreeing
Do you really think so?
I'm sorry, but I just can't accept that.
That's ridiculous/impossible.
You can't be serious.

2 Procedure
  a A chairperson from the class will open the panel discussion and invite representatives from each side to speak. Give each side a time limit.
  b Invite questions and comments from the rest of the class.
  c Take a vote on which side was most convincing.
  d The chairperson should make a few concluding remarks.

3 a In pairs write a plan for an essay *Do Near Death Experiences really exist?*

Structure it like this and make brief notes about what you will include under each

heading, using the ideas put forward at the debate.

    i   Introduction (background - what they are, and why they're important).
    ii The case for.
    iii The case against.
    iv Your own opinion and conclusion.

  b Compare your plans in groups and decide on the best set of notes.

HOMEWORK

Write the essay. Remember to express your ideas clearly and concisely and use linking words (*and/but/however*, etc.) to connect sentences and paragraphs together.

UNIT 5 THE UNCONSCIOUS MIND

13 The Unconscious Mind

1 What do you do when you're thinking about something, or talking on the phone?

Do you:
play with your hair?
tap your foot?
bite your nails?
draw something?
What else?

2 Psychologists often use doodles - those funny little drawings or lines most people seem to do when we are thinking of something else - to understand behaviour patterns. Because doodles are written unconsciously they often bring to the surface hidden areas of your mind and reveal emotion that may have been suppressed.

  a Try to remember the sort of doodle you often do and draw it on a piece of paper.
  b Which of the ones below is the most similar? (If any!)
  c Read the definitions below and match them to the doodles.

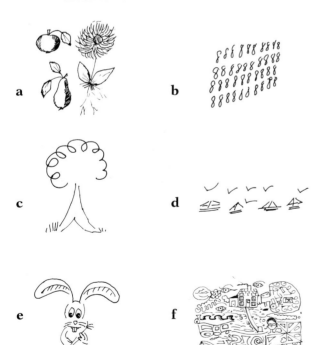

WHAT DOES IT MEAN?

1 Doodling birds, as above, demonstrates a practical disposition. When they are in the form of a v-shape they show imagination and a flair for seeking new horizons.

2 This complex doodle is a complete wish fulfilment. The house with its tiny windows, path and garden represents a strong desire for harmony, home, family and security. But the mazes and whirls reveal underlying unhappiness. You are seeking a way out of a cluttered situation in your life. A watching eye is symbolic of suspicion and jealousy.

3 Furry animals and creatures signify a love of nature and harmony. These doodles show an avoidance of friction - you are spontaneous and happy go lucky. You enjoy giving and receiving love and also have a very warm, caring personality.

4 A tree with a soft, fluffy crown indicates that you have a friendly, kindly nature, but the thin trunk shows that your feet are also on the ground and that you have a balance between head and heart. The flaring roots show excellent powers of observation.

5 A repetitive doodle scribbled over and over again, such as the one above, reveals caution and a careful, logical mind. You are consistent and don't like to commit yourself too easily in the emotional sphere. You are loyal, devoted and reliable in your friendships and relationships - but just a little dull.

6 Filling in and shading reveal a troubled mind. Plants, flowers and leaves are fertility symbols, non aggressive, but if you have filled them in or shaded them, this might indicate that you're feeling angry and pessimistic. You need to expand your creative talents and cease brooding. You show considerable artistic flair which should be directed into positive thinking.

UNIT 5 THE UNCONSCIOUS MIND — LESSON 13

d Is the doodle which is most similar to yours correct about your personality?

3 a Which doodle shows that the person is:

i suspicious, jealous and unhappy?
ii caring, warm and spontaneous?
iii balanced and observant?

b What are the nouns used in the text to correspond to these adjectives? Practise saying the word with the correct stress.

Example *sus'picion* (the stress is on the second syllable).

c Which doodle indicates:
i anger, pessimism, creativity?
ii consistency, care, logic, loyalty, devotion, reliability, dullness?
iii spontaneity, warmth?

d What are the adjectives in the text which correspond to these nouns?

Example *angry*.

e Put the adjectives above (a and b) in three columns according to whether they are **positive**, **negative** or **neutral**. Discuss what you put in each column.

Example

positive	negative	neutral
warm	*dull*	*practical*

4 Here are three more doodles. What do you think they show about the personalities of the people they were drawn by? Read the notes about the basic points to look for to help you.

Basic points to look for:

Upward strokes indicate intellectual and even spiritual aspirations.
Downward strokes show emotional influences and creativity.
Firm pressure is a sign of energy and conflict.
Light pressure reveals sensitivity and receptivity but also touchiness.
Angular doodles indicate aggression and also planning ability.
Rounded or curved strokes show affection, friendliness and sentimentality.
Filling in or shading shows tension and insecurity.
Underlining or little boxes indicate a sense of protection and desire for security. The doodler may be feeling trapped.
Movements to the right are pointing to the outside world and people; to the left they signify introversion.

a Listen to what the 'expert' says on the tape. First decide which doodle you think she is talking about and then write notes on what she says about the type of person.

b How near were you to what she said?

HOMEWORK

Ask someone to draw a doodle for you and then write a description of their personality, based on the information above. Add a paragraph which assesses how accurate you think it is.

UNIT 5 THE UNCONSCIOUS MIND

14 To Sleep...

1 Discuss these questions and compare your answers, giving reasons where relevant.

a Have you ever been unable to sleep? If so, what do you do to help you?
b Do you read a book or have a drink when you go to bed?
c Do you sleep with your window open or closed?
d Do you prefer a hard or a soft bed?
e Are you a 'night owl' or an 'early bird'?
f How many hours a night do you try to sleep?

2 Discover what your sleeping position says about your personality.

a Look at these pictures. In which of them is the person:

i stretched out on her back with legs apart?
ii curled up in a ball?
iii flat on her stomach?
iv on her side?

b Which of the positions do you think show that you are:

i trusting, kind and sensitive and often feel guilty?
ii nervous, easily hurt and shy?
iii outspoken, decisive and cautious?
iv sociable, secretive and a worrier?

Check the definitions and see if you were correct.

Position One: The Human Ball
You tuck yourself up into a tight ball-classically known as the 'foetal position' since this is the position that a baby assumes when still in its mother's womb. By nature you're nervous and shy. You bring your knees up towards your chest and aren't above putting a thumb nail into your mouth. You're defensive and easily hurt. You may be an only child - you've learnt you have to rely on yourself a good deal. You also have a low opinion of yourself.

Position Two: Well Balanced
You usually sleep on one side. You tend to be able to make rational decisions fairly quickly. You know most of your strengths - and weaknesses. You're fairly cautious when you meet new people. You've had too many unhappy experiences to make the same old mistakes again. You occasionally suffer from anxiety but only rarely from depression. You're fairly outspoken and don't worry much about annoying people you think have done something wrong.

UNIT 5 THE UNCONSCIOUS MIND   LESSON 14

Position Three: Vulnerable
You lie flat on your back in bed. Your legs are probably apart and your arms can be anywhere. You're a very trusting, vulnerable, open sort of person. You hardly ever say what you really mean - because you don't like the idea of upsetting anyone. You are shy, often susceptible to guilty feelings, and tend to lack confidence in yourself and your own abilities. You have a low opinion of yourself and tend to be easily convinced by new arguments or theories.

Position Four: Protective
You lie on your stomach - often with your head resting on an arm. You are rather secretive and defensive and tend to take umbrage easily. You worry a lot and brood if people say things that upset you. You cry easily and get upset at the slightest things. But, to balance that, you do find it easy to enjoy yourself. You enjoy meeting people and having a good time. You're not over ambitious and tend to live for today rather than worry too much about the future.

3
a   Which position do you usually sleep in? Is the definition of your character correct?
b   Make a list of new adjectives from the text. Check the meaning in a dictionary and put the words in columns depending on whether you think they are **positive**, **negative** or **neutral**.
c   Discuss why you put the words in the columns you did.

positive	negative	neutral
decisive	*anxious*	*cautious*

4   Answer the following questions based on the text.

When you go to bed tonight you'll probably lie awake for a few minutes before you fall asleep. Once you've managed to relax and get rid of the physical tensions and accumulated mental cares of the day, you'll slowly become more and more drowsy.
Then you'll drift first into a fairly light sleep and then into a deep sleep that will last for between 30 and 60 minutes. This whole pattern of drowsiness, light sleep and deep sleep lasts for around 90 minutes before it starts all over again.
During an average night's sleep you'll go through this cycle four or five times. But after the first cycle each new cycle begins not with a period of drowsiness, but with a special type of sleep known as Rapid Eye Movement or REM sleep, because while you're in it your eyes will move rapidly below your closed lids. REM sleep lasts for between 10 and 30 minutes at a time and it's during REM sleep that you enter dreamland - an insane, unstructured world where there are no rules and no constraints, where nothing is impossible and where the limits of your imagination are pushed beyond infinity.

a   What is the usual pattern of sleep?
b   How long does it last?
c   What is REM and how long does it last?
d   When do you dream?

HOMEWORK

Keep a 'dream diary' for a week and see if there are any recurrent themes. Use the extract below to help you.

YOUR DREAMS CAN HELP YOU

Your dreams can tell you a lot about the inner workings of your mind. If you have difficulty in remembering your dreams;
write down what you do remember - you'll find that as you write things down, more and more details will become clear;
keep your notebook and pencil by the side of your bed so that you can write your dreams down with getting up - the more you move about, the quicker the memories of your dreams will disappear;
don't strain too much to remember a dream - if you chase a dream it will become as elusive as a rainbow;
if you find it difficult to write down your dreams try drawing or painting the images.

UNIT 5   THE UNCONSCIOUS MIND

15 ...Perchance to Dream

1 Read through these extracts which describe various dreams and try to explain them.

a Make up a title for three of the dreams.

b Do any of these dreams seem familiar to you?

1 Dreams about death and dying needn't necessarily be gloomy and depressing. If you dream that you are dying then you may simply be looking forward to a new beginning, rebirth, a new life. Perhaps you are about to start a stimulating new job or maybe a new personal relationship has just begun. If you dream that someone who is close to you is dying, then that may suggest you are going to separate - perhaps only temporarily, perhaps more permanently. A dream about being buried may mean you feel that you are being held back or 'buried' by drudgery or daily responsibilities. You may feel that you are being dominated or repressed by someone.

2 Dreams about boats are common place. To learn anything from your dream you must remember a little more about the boat. Was it floating happily and comfortably? Were you enjoying yourself? If so, that suggests you're happy with your life. But if the boat was sinking or leaking than you may feel 'all at sea'.

3 You can see it in the distance it starts to move out of the station. You run faster. The train starts to pick up speed. You are running as fast you can move. You reach out. You just manage to grasp the door handle. You open the train door. You're about to climb aboard. But the train has picked up too much speed. You cannot get aboard, and are left standing on the platform. Breathless, you stand and watch as the train pulls away without you.

The train can, of course, be a plane, bus or boat. What does it mean? It is, after all, a common enough dream experience. It can mean several things: that you don't have confidence in a current plan or project. It can mean that you are worried about failure ('missing the boat'). Or it can mean that in your heart you may feel that a current project is not worth all the effort. Do you want to 'get away from it all'- or would you really rather things stayed as they are? If you catch the train (or boat, or bus, or plane) then you are probably feeling fairly confident about your plans for the future.

4 If your dream is populated with famous people - film stars, television celebrities and well - known politicians - there can often be many possible explanations. It may be that you would like to move in more exciting circles. Perhaps you find your present life rather drab and uninteresting. Maybe you would like to add a little sparkle to your normal daily activities. Your exciting dream may be nothing more than a pleasant form of fantasy escapism. How did you respond to the famous people? If you treated them as equals then that suggests your self-confidence is high. But if you felt inferior, your self-esteem is low.

2 Look more carefully at the extracts. Which dream indicates that:

a you are worried about failing at something you are doing?
b you are afraid of being separated from somebody you are close to?
c you are happy?
d you would like your life to be more exciting?

3 Find a word or phrase which means:

a depressing (1)
b pushed under (1)
c go below the surface (2)
d letting water in (2)
e go faster (3)
f take hold firmly (3)
g dull (4)
h excitement (4)

4 a Listen to four people talking about dreams they have had and make notes on what they say.

b Work in pairs. Student A should choose two of the dreams described in the listening text. Student B is a psychologist, and he or she will give Student A advice based on what Student A says about his/her dream. This advice will be based on what is in the reading texts.

HOMEWORK

Follow the suggestions below and see if you can manipulate your dreams to do what you want. Continue to keep your 'dream diary' and see if what you dream reflects the aim you set yourself when you go to sleep. Report what happens in one of the following lessons.

CHOOSE YOUR DREAMS

Dream researchers have found that many people can choose what they dream about. All you have to do to dictate the content of your dream, is to concentrate on the scene or individual that you'd like to dream about. And as you fall asleep, try to make sure that the last thing on your mind is the thing you want to dream about. But there is one snag. Although you may be able to decide the basic content of your dream, you won't be able to plan what happens! And remember, too, that in dreamland there are no rules. In your dreams the dead can speak and the living can fly. Your plans for a night of passion with the superstar hero of your dreams could easily turn into something very different...

UNIT 6 YOUNG PEOPLE TODAY

16 Hopes for the Future

1 a The following article is the results of a survey done with 11-15 year old British teenagers. By looking at the headline try and predict what they said about:

jobs   family life   holidays

QUIET, SECURE LIFE IS GOAL FOR CHILDREN

b Read the text quickly and see if you were correct.

Were you surprised by anything which was said?
Do you think this is very different to what this age-group in your country would say?

c The interviewer asked nine questions to get the information he required.

i What were these questions and which paragraphs do they refer to?
ii Compare your questions in groups.

---

1   TEENAGERS want well-paid jobs, a cosy family life and good health, and would prefer to spend a quiet night at home in front of the television to going out on the town, according to a survey of 13,000 youngsters. Most boys - 25 per cent - wanted to become managers or businessmen, while the same number of girls looked forward to being nurses or teachers. Only eight per cent of the girls wanted to be engineers or scientists, and three per cent of males wanted to become teachers or nurses. The survey showed a majority of both sexes expected to be earning between £20,000 and £30,000 a year by the time they are 30. Asked about their choices for holidays, 65 per cent said they would rather relax on a Caribbean island than ski in the Alps, party in St Tropez or trek in the Himalayas. The Australian soap opera Neighbours easily topped the teenage television ratings.

2   For boys, the most popular way of spending an 'ideal evening' - for 29 per cent - was a 'quiet night by the telly with my partner' rather than an elegant dinner party, a visit to a disco or wine bar, or an outing to the cinema or theatre. Girls were keener to go out - and staying in to watch television was the last thing they wanted to do. Swimming was the most popular sport for both sexes, although football was the favourite for boys. Skiing was the sport that both sexes would take up if they had the chance, with American football second choice for the boys and water skiing for the girls. From a choice of 20 'heroes', most boys said they would like to be Daley Thompson while the girls picked the pop star Madonna. A total of 67 per cent of the youngsters expected to be married and with children by the age of 30. However, more than a third did not want children at that age, and 20 per cent thought they would stay single. The survey also showed that cruelty to animals, education and famine were the issues young teenagers cared most about. While 90 per cent of girls said they cared at least a little for equality for women, 24 per cent of boys said they did not care at all.

UNIT 6 YOUNG PEOPLE TODAY — LESSON 16

2 a Find a word or expression in the text which means the following. The letters are jumbled up:
i   warm and comfortable   yocs
ii to have a good time   no eht wtno
iii wait for, with pleasure   lkoo wdroafr ot
iv list of most popular things   gtasnri
v   question for discussion   seusi

b ALSO and AND are linking expressions which add two parts of a sentence to each other. Look at the tapescript and find three linking expressions which contrast ideas.

3 You are going to listen to Beatrice, who comes from Argentina, talking about the differences between life as a teenager in her country compared to Britain.

a What can you guess she is going to say about the following topics?

social life
marriage and the opposite sex
family life
smoking and drinking
music
clothes

b Listen to what Beatrice says and number the topics above in the order she speaks about them.

Were your guesses about what she was going to say correct?

c Decide whether the following statements are true or false, according to what Beatrice said.

i   Grandparents are the only people the teenagers respect.
ii   Argentinian teenagers always wear the latest fashions.
iii They prefer colours that are not too bright.
iv   They like the same kind of music as in Britain and the United States.
v   The teenagers get bored with their social life.
vi   Parties have to finish before midnight.
vii Marriage is no longer so popular.

d Discuss any differences between the life-style of a teenager in Argentina and in your country.

4 a Think of questions that you would like to ask teenagers in your country about their life-style. Use the reading and listening texts in this lesson to give you ideas.

b Build up a list of questions and decide which ones are the best by comparing them in groups.

HOMEWORK

Ask your questions to a few teenagers in your country and then write a short survey, using the model you read earlier. Use expressions of quantity (most, 30 per cent, etc.) and linking expressions (also, however, etc.) and contrast the life of teenagers in your country with what you know about the life of teenagers in Britain. Invent a title for your piece of writing.

UNIT 6 YOUNG PEOPLE TODAY

17 Teenagers Now

1 The following text is one of the entries for a competition which asked for a short extract, or poem, or diary, or play around the theme of teenagers today. It was written by a 16 year old girl.

   a Discuss what things you would expect a 16 year old to write about, and then read the text.

TEENAGERS NOW

'They seem to grow up so quickly these days' is commonly on adult lips, followed by, 'When I was young' and a tirade of which the main line of argument seems to be that not only was life much harder, but that everyone did a better job of living it! It seems to me, however, that there can be no objective discussion as no one is a teenager twice.

The young of today do have problems. They are considered adults long before their parents were. This removes the frustration of not being taken seriously or respected, and allows much more freedom. Unfortunately, it often makes life harder because teenagers are not adults. Although they look and act like adults, they lack experience and so often make mistakes which people don't understand or tolerate. Unfortunately, the family is not such a strong and supportive unit as it was. One-parent families are common and mothers often work, either because they have to or because they wish to have a 'career'. This means that children and teenagers receive less care and time, and this lack of parental input leads to many teenagers dropping out and not working. 'Mothering' is no longer recognised as the most important and difficult job there is, and this in turn devalues children and teenagers.

Young people start to dress and look like adults at an early age and so come into contact with drugs, cigarettes, alcohol and sex earlier. The permissive society that we live in now is very contradictory and difficult to contend with. It is also so changed that parents have no idea of the pressures put on the young by their peers and so cannot help them. AIDS is a new threat, but perhaps will help teenagers as it will prevent them from 'sleeping around' and so losing much self-respect. It might also give them an unquestionable reason for saying 'no'.

If you conclude, as I have, that adolescence is harder now than it was for our parents, it might also be recognised that being a parent is also now more difficult.

Emma Fergusson (16)

   b Decide if the following statements are true or false according to Emma.

     i *Adults seem to think that life was more difficult for them when they were young.*
     ii *Adults think teenagers coped better in their day.*
     iii *Teenagers have more freedom these days.*
     iv *They often do not behave like adults.*
     v *Parents often do not give as much time to their children as they used to.*

2 Do you agree with the following comments which Emma made? Think about these points and discuss them in groups, giving examples from your own experience where possible.

   a *One parent families and working mothers mean that children and teenagers receive less care and time.*
   b *Teenagers often 'drop out' and don't work because of this lack of attention from their parents.*
   c *Lack of 'mothering' devalues children and teenagers.*
   d *The permissive society we live in is very contradictory and difficult to contend with.*
   e *Parents have no idea of the pressures put on the young by their peers and so cannot help them.*
   f *Being a parent is now also more difficult.*

UNIT 6 YOUNG PEOPLE TODAY — LESSON 17

3 Listen to this interview with an 87 year old woman, Mrs Lawson.

  a Which of the following things does she talk about? Select them, and put them in the order in which she talks about them.

  freedom of teenagers today
  being punished
  clothes
  relationship between parents and children
  where she would go when she went out
  being an only child
  pocket money
  wearing makeup
  going out with friends
  drinking and smoking

  b Listen again.

  ii Make notes about what she said, under the headings that you ticked.
  iii Compare your notes with someone else.

4 Discuss the way in which you and your brothers and/or sisters, if you have any, were brought up. In what ways were your parents good parents? Did they make any mistakes? In what ways would you be different if you had children?

5 Imagine you were entering a competition which required you to produce a piece of creative writing around the theme of 'Teenagers Today'. It could be from the point of view of a parent, teacher or old person, as well as from a teenager's perspective. It could be (among other things) a short extract, a poem, a letter, a diary extract or a story. Work individually or with another student to produce a piece of writing. It could either be imaginary or from your own experience.

HOMEWORK

Interview an old person about their life as a teenager and how it compared with the life of a teenager today. Report back in the next lesson.

UNIT 6 YOUNG PEOPLE TODAY

18 A Question of Class?

1 How important are the following to you? Put them in order of priority and discuss with others.

- education and an interesting career
- money and a high standard of living
- relationships: marriage/family life love/friends
- social life

2 The two articles below are both interviews with 19 year old British women, Emma and Sharon.

a Half the class will read the interview with Emma and the other half of the class will read the interview with Sharon.

b Write down the main topic(s) discussed in each paragraph. Then compare what you have written with someone else.

3 Look again at the text you read and do the relevant vocabulary activity below. Many of the expressions in the text are colloquial. Find words or expressions which mean:

EMMA

Emma Rowlands, 19, was brought up in Derby. She was educated at a private high school for girls and left with 12 O levels and four A levels. She is now living in Sheffield studying medicine at the university. She lives in a student house with three other girls but spends the holidays with her parents. She is an only child.

1 'When I was younger my biggest worry was being a teenager and my biggest ambition was to get my A levels - I didn't want to end up working in Woolworths. Now, as long as I pass everything, I shouldn't have any worries because I'm doing what I want to do. I think that if I hadn't gone to university, I wouldn't have been able to get a job worth having. Your choices widen as you become more educated, and if I hadn't got a place first time, I would have tried again and again until I was accepted. My parents have been role models for me. They went to university and so I never even considered anything else.'

2 But life at university isn't all work, no play. 'My social life varies depending on my mood. I like to go for a quiet drink or perhaps for a meal or to the theatre. I just love relaxing with my friends, talking and discussing. However much money I had, an ideal night out would still be to go and see a really good play and then go out for a meal.' Emma likes reading, jogging, swimming and playing water polo and squash. She admits that her friends are not not varied. 'The people I'm closest to are all from the same background. It didn't happen by chance. I just attracted the people most like me.'

On the whole, Emma feels indebted to her parents for the way she has grown up. 'They have always treated me like a human being with opinions and feelings and I think their entire outlook throughout my upbringing has been very liberal. I would say that my mother is probably my best friend.' But when it comes to boyfriends, Emma has different ideas from her mother, who got married when she was 19.

3 'The biggest thing I've learnt is that I wouldn't marry so early. You should definitely live with a person before you marry them and I think the ideal age to marry is 29, so that you can have some time as a couple before having children at about 36. The first time I went out with a boy was when I was 16. I think my parents would only express concern about a boy if he was a lot older.'

4 When it comes to clothes, Emma likes to dress in a classical but practical way. 'I'm very fond of buying clothes and I like to be smart. I'm not keen on places like Chelsea Girl and Top Shop and I only ever buy things that I know I'm going to wear and wear.' Emma, who is an avid Neighbours fan, has some strong views about TV in general. 'I think watching telly shows a lack of imagination. It's like being child surrounded by toys who still needs someone to play with.'

5 As well as Neighbours, Emma also watches the news. She reads the Sunday Times and the Daily Telegraph and at the last election she voted SDP.

6 Emma's ideal holiday is a cultural one and if offered all the money in the world, she still wouldn't go to the Caribbean: 'You can get the same sun rays on the same textured beach in Spain for a lot less money,' she says practically. Dream holidays aside, when it comes to her dream...'Everybody wants to live in the country, have a farm and a bit of land at the back.'

7 Emma thinks English people are odd and very eccentric, as well as being friendly. 'The aristocracy will always exist, although the barriers are less strong than they were after the war. In America, if people see someone driving a Rolls Royce, they think great, whereas here they'd rather scratch a key across it.'

8 No doubt happy with her lifestyle, Emma's sketch of the future is solid: 'By the time I'm 40 I hope to have had my litter and be fairly well off with emotional and financial security. By the time you're 35 you really should be going places.'

UNIT 6 YOUNG PEOPLE TODAY — LESSON 18

SHARON

Sharon Dole, 19, lives in Essex in a new town just outside Chelmsford. She left her North London comprehensive at the age of 16 with two O levels and now works as a hairdresser earning an average of £70 a week.

1 'When I was 12 my biggest ambition was to leave home by the time I was 16 and to have a Porsche by the time I was 17. From the age of 14 I knew I wanted to be a hairdresser.

2 Tempted by the dosh, Sharon's biggest ambition now is to have her own chain of hairdressing salons.

3 Going to university was never high up on Sharon's list of priorities. 'I used to think that school was like a prison.' But what is high up on the list is boys. 'I've been boy crazy since I was 12, when I started going out with my first boyfriend. Since then I've had hundreds of them, I've lost count.'

4 As for her actual views on boys, she doesn't rate them highly. 'All blokes like to lie. They tell girls how they're beautiful and how madly in love they are. I think you should just have a laugh and then get rid of them.' And as for marriage? 'I'd like to get married when I'm about 25. If my last boyfriend had asked me, I'd have jumped at the chance. I'd like the engagement to last a long time and I wouldn't live with him before because then there's no point: it just becomes a piece of paper.'

5 For Sharon, an average night out is going to the disco. 'There are discos everywhere in Essex and on a Saturday night I always make sure I'm not in before 2am. When I was younger my parents used to make me be in by 10.30 during the week.'

6 When Sharon's not down the disco, she spends a lot of her time cutting people's hair and trying to renovate her Fiat Super Mirafiori. 'I'm not interested in current affairs, I think it's all boring and I'm not at all religious. I used to read The Sun but now if I want to know the news, I just listen to other people or watch the telly. On the whole I don't watch much telly. I prefer listening to records and I absolutely idolise Duran Duran. As for fashion, I don't wear what everyone else wears. I dress for sexuality and what I feel comfortable in. When I go shopping I spend lots of money on leather. I love it. I paid £190 for one of my jackets.'

7 Sharon goes away on holiday once a year with a friend in August. 'I usually go to Majorca but this year I'm going to Tenerife. I like a holiday with lots and lots of nightlife. If I had loads of money, I'd go to Malibu and get a house next door to Rob Lowe so that I could sit there and stare. The furthest I've been is Portugal.'

8 For the future, Sharon wants to avoid doing what her mother did... I don't think she's lived her life to the full. I want to enjoy my life even more than I have already.'

Emma
- a different (para 2)
- b In general (para 2)
- c attitude (para 2)
- d enthusiastic (para 4)
- e rich (para 8)

Sharon
- f money (para 2)
- g a lot of (para 3)
- h men (para 4)
- i make yourself free of them (para 4)

Read the text you didn't read in class, together with the vocabulary activity and make a note of any useful vocabulary.

4 Look carefully at your text and write down notes about:
- a her education, and attitude to it
- b her job
- c her social life
- d her attitude to men and marriage
- e what clothes she likes wearing
- f her attitude to current affairs/TV/newspapers
- g her ideal holiday
- h her ambitions for the future
- i her ideal night out

5 Work with someone who has read the interview you have not read and find out what the differences are between Sharon and Emma.
- a Why do you think there are such great differences between the two girls? How many of the differences are because of the difference in social class? Would it be the same in your country?
- b Do you identify more with Sharon or Emma? Why?

6 Ask someone in the class who you don't know very well the questions above, and make notes.

7 Write a short summary of the interview in a mixture of direct and indirect speech, in the style of the written texts. Don't put the person's name on it and see if the rest of the class can guess who it is.

HOMEWORK

Read the text you didn't read in class, together with the vocabulary activity and make a note of any useful vocabulary.

UNIT 7 TROPICAL PARADISE?

19 Describing Places

1 Look at this picture of Bali, a popular holiday destination in Indonesia.

   a What do you know about Bali?
   b What sort of place do you think it is?
   c Write down some words that you associate with it.

2 Look at the words below and match the categories **a** to **i** to the details **i** to **ix**.

   a climate
   b cultural interest
   c religion
   d things to see
   e geographical location
   f crops
   g vegetation
   h size
   i wildlife

   i to the South of the main island
   ii exotic parrots
   iii Muslim
   iv local dances
   v jungle
   vi 300 kilometres from North to South
   vii ancient palaces
   viii rice
   ix temperate

3 **a** Choose descriptive words or phrases to describe your own country, using the same categories in the left-hand column above. Add any other categories you can think of. For example: population, industry, history.

   b Compare your ideas in groups.

4 Look at these three extracts which give information about Bali. Match the extracts to their sources.
   a travel brochure
   b encyclopedia
   c guide book

UNIT 7 TROPICAL PARADISE? LESSON 19

1 For many westerners, Bali doesn't extend beyond the tourist leaflet: idyllic tropical beaches, lush green forests and happy islanders who work and play in childlike innocence. This vision of paradise has been turned into a commodity for the tens of thousands of western tourists who flood into Bali's Kuta Beach every year, who see nothing but Kuta Beach, and go away leaving the sand scarred end to end with motorcycle tracks. In actual fact the tourist trade is only a peripheral thing; away from the commercial traps of the southern beaches you can still find Bali's soul, towards the mountains where it has always been. It is there you will find rice paddies tripping down hillsides like giant steps, holy mountains reaching up through the clouds, dense tropical jungles, long sandy beaches, warm blue water and crashing surf. And it's there you'll discover the extraordinary resilience of the Balinese people and their culture.

2 The very name of Bali conveys an aura of magic, and this island paradise amply fulfils all expectations. One of the reasons for Bali's position as Indonesia's number one tourist destination is undoubtedly its great scenic beauty - majestic mountains, tranquil lakes, lush green rice terraces and glorious beaches - but it's the unique charm of the Balinese themselves which makes a holiday in Bali so unforgettable. Their deep religious beliefs permeate every aspect of their daily lives, and are instilled in all their ancient ways - the grace and beauty of their dance, the joy of their music, the colour and spectacle of their ceremony, their innate skills as artists and craftsmen, and their extraordinary hospitality and friendliness. Bali's constant sunshine, combined with its rich, unending variety of new sights and experiences, will cast a spell on you to last a lifetime.

3 BALI

one of the Lesser Sunda islands, east of Java, 90 ml in length and with a maximum width of 50 ml. A chain of volcanic mountains crosses the island from west to east, the highest peak being Goenoeng Agoeng, (10,309 ft). South of these mountains is a triangular-shaped plain, bordered southwards by the limestone Tafelhoek peninsula. The fertile volcanic ash soils of the plain are intensively cultivated with rice, maize, coffee and coconuts. Irrigation is widely used. The Balinese are akin to, though of generally finer physique than, the Javanese. Their religion is a form of Hinduism. They are famed for their intricate forms of dancing and for their skill in working metals and wood. Bali, with Lombok, forms a separate residency, partly governed by native rulers. The capital of the Lesser Sunda islands is Den Pasar in Bali. Other towns are Singaraja, Kloenkoeng and Boeleleng. Pop. (1930) 1,101,393.

J.C.S

5 Imagine you are writing a travel advertisement for Bali to go with the picture above. What adjectives could you put before the following nouns to make them sound really attractive?

mountains	beaches
people	food
rice terraces	sunshine

Compare your adjectives with the ones used in extracts 1 and 2 in **4**.

6 Write a similar extract about your own country. Include as many of the categories and descriptive words and phrases as you can. Compare with the other groups.

HOMEWORK

Write two descriptions of a place you know or have spent a holiday in. One description should be factual (like a guidebook or an encyclopedia) and the other should be more persuasive, such as an advertisement in a holiday brochure.

UNIT 7 TROPICAL PARADISE?

20 Selling Tourism

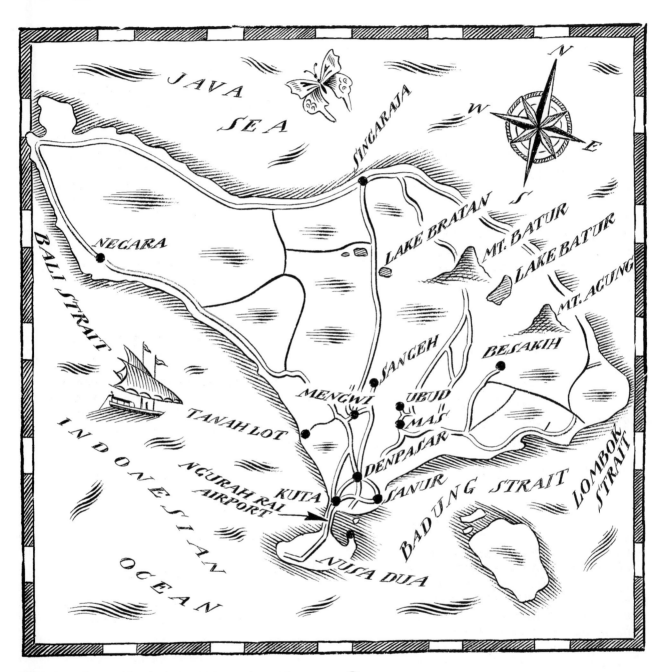

1 Listen to Sarah talking about her holiday in Bali. As you listen to the first extract make a note of the places she visited and what she did there. Use the map to help you.

2 This is an extract from the brochure that originally persuaded her to book her holiday on Bali.

Read the text once and then listen to the second extract, where Sarah describes her holiday. Make a list of the differences between what was advertised in the brochure and what the holiday was really like.

UNIT 7 TROPICAL PARADISE? LESSON 20

A HOLIDAY IN PARADISE

Have you ever been tempted by a tropical island holiday? Have you ever felt like stretching out on white sands under azure skies to feel a gentle sea breeze play in your hair while you listen to the gentle lapping of the sea? Have you ever dreamed of being able to combine all this with fascinating sights, smiling locals famous for their hospitality as well as eating exotic food such as beef cooked in coconut and spices or fresh lobster grilled on the beach? Or what about spicy salads with traditional peanut sauce?

All this is now possible at astonishingly low prices! Bali awaits you this summer and it won't cost you the Earth if you take advantage of our amazingly priced special deal.

You will be accommodated in 'Longboat Cottages' - a hotel with every modern convenience you could think of, including a spacious swimming pool with poolside bar, tennis courts, restaurants, a fitness centre, a shopping mall and an evening barbecue area. Swimming in the sea is made easy with access to Sanur Beach close by. There you can swim in the clear sparkling water and lie on the golden sands under the swaying palm trees. Peaceful, unspoilt Kuta beach is also a short walk away from the hotel. When you can tear yourself away from the beach you will find that a delightfully traditional straw roofed cottage awaits you - together, of course, with private bathroom.

Can you resist this holiday of a lifetime? You will be the envy of your friends when you show them the wood-carvings, puppets and leather goods which are only some of the traditional articles made on this breathtakingly beautiful island.

This offer is ONLY available through Grant Tours.

Holidays are for 2 or 3 weeks - starting at the ridiculously low price of only £699, which includes return flight, accommodation and half board.

Why not ring today for a full colour brochure and booking form: 0223 487321.

Or write for further details to:

Bali Offer
Grant Tours Ltd
135 King's Street
Cambridge

HURRY - LIMITED NUMBER OF PLACES ARE AVAILABLE!

3 a Find as many examples as you can in the brochure of language which is typically persuasive or exaggerated 'selling' language of advertisements.

   Example *astonishingly low prices*

   b Find as many examples as you can in the brochure of purely factual language. For **Example** *holidays are for 2 or 3 weeks*

4 a Write a similar holiday brochure intended to try to persuade people to go to a place you know. It could be a place you have lived in, or a place that you have been to on holiday. Make it sound as attractive as possible, and include illustrations if you can.

   b Present your advertisement to the class and be prepared to answer questions on it.

HOMEWORK

When Sarah returned from her holiday in Bali she wrote a letter of complaint to the travel agent in which she complained about the inaccuracies in the holiday brochure.

Write Sarah's letter, using phrases like:

although ... in fact ...

it said that ... but in reality ...

it is claimed that ... However, ...

Say what the differences were, how you felt about it, and what you think the travel agent should do.

UNIT 7 TROPICAL PARADISE?

21 The Future of the Island

1 Some tourist resorts have been developed to such an extent that a lot of people complain that the area has been 'spoiled'. What do people mean by this? Can you give some examples of the way that an attractive area can become spoiled?

Work with another student and make a list of the examples.

2 Now listen to a radio talk about the bad effects of tourism on the island of Bali, and fill in the gaps in this newspaper article, which summarises the main problems facing the island today.

46

UNIT 7 TROPICAL PARADISE?   LESSON 21

The increasing number of tourists (from _____ **a** _____ and, more recently from _____ **b** _____) coming to Bali has brought some benefits; better roads, an improved _____ **c** _____ and a better _____ **d** _____ service. People on Bali have a higher standard of living than the rest of _____ **e** _____ . It has also helped some people to make money; particularly shopkeepers, ___ **f** ___ drivers and _____ **g** _____ . However some of the residents of Bali are getting angry about some of the negative aspects that tourism brings. Not only do tourists pollute the island with noise and litter but there have also been increasing reports of people taking _____ **h** _____. Drunkenness and topless _____ **i** _____ are other complaints high on the residents' list and the police are worried about _____ **j** _____ such as mugging, _____ **k** _____ and prostitution. The island is also becoming well known for its 'hard sell'. One person we spoke to complained that he was accosted no fewer than _____ **l** _____ times by youngsters wanting to _____ **m** _____ something, or by old ladies _____ **n** _____ _____ a massage. Is the traditional lifestyle and its unique culture going to disappear and will tourists continue to go to Bali if the situation doesn't improve?

3   Role Play

The local residents have called a meeting to voice their worries about the situation regarding tourism on their island, and to invite and give proposals about what should happen in the future. They have invited the following people to be present:

a foreign tourist
a local hotel owner (who is making money from tourism)
a representative of the local residents
a government official (acting as chairperson)
a foreign tour operator
a journalist (to take minutes)

Procedure

Planning meeting

Have a 'planning meeting' when each group of representatives will decide what you are going to say and what action you want to take/to be taken. Then appoint a spokesperson to represent you (look at the appropriate rolecard below, but you should use your imagination as much as possible). Don't look at your rolecard during the roleplay. The class will be divided into six groups, representing each person present. You will all decide what is to be said at the meeting, but only one of you will actually speak (the others will listen to the discussion and ask for questions or clarification).

Meeting

- The chairperson should open the meeting by introducing the local residents' representative and asking him/her to explain why they called the meeting.

- Each of the other groups should be introduced and will have three minutes to explain their point of view and give their suggestions. The chairperson can also participate (the journalist will not speak, but can ask questions).

- The chairperson should ask for questions or clarification.

- Each group should be asked to give a brief summary.

- The chairperson should make a list of points which all representatives will agree on and ensure that there are some definite decisions.

- The journalist should read out the minutes.

LESSON 21 — UNIT 8 TROPICAL PARADISE?

3 Role Cards

1 A foreign tourist
You have been coming here regularly for many years but in the past few years you have noticed that:
- prices have increased dramatically
- the island is getting dirtier
- the locals are not nearly so friendly
- traditional food and entertainment is being replaced by international hamburgers, discos, etc.

2 A local hotel owner
- your hotel gives pleasure to foreign visitors
- you provide jobs for lots of local people
- you have been making money from the hotel trade but you have invested a lot of it in your hotel
- you want to encourage tourists to continue coming so that you can open a new hotel next year
- if tourists didn't come to Bali they would go somewhere else
- you believe we must give tourists what they want

3 Local Residents' representative
The residents in the tourist parts of Bali (mainly in the south) have been complaining about:
- the high prices in shops and restaurants, which they can't afford
- he dirt and litter which is everywhere
- the noise late at night from bars, discos, motor bikes and so on
- the decline in the standard of education and the discipline in schools
- the decline in moral standards (drink, drugs, prostitution - general corruption)
- the gradual disappearance of cultural traditions and values
- a lot of the food and drink for the tourists is imported, so this doesn't help the local economy

4 A government official
You have to act as chairperson. This means you have to open the meeting and make sure that everyone has the opportunity to speak, but does not monopolise the discussion. Use formal language, such as *I call on the representative of the local residents to speak*. You must ensure that some decisions are made by the end of the meeting.
- You are also allowed to participate. You have the following government information:
- Bali has been making a lot of money from tourism. Because of this, several developmental programmes have taken place
- government figures show that tourism has doubled over the last three years
- the rate of inflation on the island has risen by 35 per cent over the same period
- last year 27 tourists were charged with drug offences - ten of these were 'hard drug' offences.

5 A foreign tour operator
You have been making a lot of money from holidays to Bali, which have been becoming increasingly popular:
- your marketing department has shown that there is expected to be increasing demand for holidays in this area
- a recent survey of customers has shown that 45 per cent of your customers stated that their holiday on Bali was the best they had ever had
- you are interested in making the residents less 'pushy' with the tourists, as this seems to be unpopular with many people. You are also interested in encouraging them to keep traditional festivals and customs, as these are a big selling point for you
- Bali needs tourism to help development
- it is better to have rich tourists than penniless hippies

6 Journalist
Keep a note of what happens during the meeting, and read out the minutes of the meeting at the end. Remember to use reporting verbs such as *...stated that/argued that/claimed* or *A different point of view was put by ... who said that...*'.

HOMEWORK

Write up the minutes of the meeting in the form of a newspaper report for a local newspaper. Give a brief summary of the meeting, and report the decisions which were made. Include a headline which will catch people's attention.

UNIT 8 EDUCATION

22 Describing Schools

1 What are the differences between the following types of British schools?

a comprehensive
b alternative
c public
d boarding

Which are state schools (paid for and controlled by the government) and which are private schools (where parents pay)?

2 Divide into three groups. Each group should read one of the articles about schools.
Group 1 read about life at a comprehensive school.
Group 2 reads about life at a public/boarding school.
Group 3 read about life at an alternative school.

a First predict, in groups, what you think the students will say about these topics. Check first that you understand what the topics mean.

School rules
Extra curricular activities
Typical daily routine
What she thinks of school

b Read the article and make notes about the headings in **a**.

c Make sure you know the exact meanings of the words listed in a box beneath the text you have read.

d Compare your answers and discuss any vocabulary problems with the rest of the group.

3 a Work with two people who have read the other articles and find out about the other two students at different schools. Make notes of:
what they do on a typical day
what they are allowed/not allowed to do
the school subjects studied
extra activities they do
what the person thinks of the school

Name: Katy Roberts
Age: 16
School: Backwell School, Backwell, Avon
Type: Comprehensive

'I'm in the fifth year at Backwell School. Like most of the 1,000 kids who come here, I travel here every morning on the school bus. I get here for 8.50am when we have to register with our tutor group. At nine the buzzer goes and we have our first two 50 minutes lessons, then a break of 20 minutes. We have two more lessons then lunch which lasts 50 minutes. I usually hang out with my friends or boyfriend at lunch, but there are lunch-time activities I could do.
'We have a 25 minute tutorial after lunch and before our next two classes, where we receive messages, chat to our tutor groups or go to assembly. Our school is strict on discipline with detentions for swearing or breaking the school rules, but the uniform's quite relaxed. We have to wear navy or black but we can wear any style we want, although if something's too fashionable, for example a brightly coloured coat, we have to take it off. I like our uniform. It's comfortable to wear and the colour's okay. The activities at school are really good - both the kids and teachers are into them. There's loads of after-school clubs and trips we can do - weight training, squash, trampolining, hockey, music lessons, orchestra, drama club, ski trips, cookery trips to France, school discos for the younger kids, charity fetes, etc. I like my school - it's friendly and my mates are here. People might think you get a better standard of schooling by paying to go to a private school, but I think Backwell has a high standard of education and a good reputation. I'd never want to go anywhere else!'

kid   tutor group   a buzzer   a break
chat   detentions   mates

LESSON 22 — UNIT 8 EDUCATION

Name: Emma Langford
Age: 17
School: Cobham Hall, Kent
Type: Public/Boarding School

'I've been going to Cobham Hall for seven years and I love it. The average day here begins at 7am when we're woken up to have breakfast. By 8.25am we have to be in our tutorial groups where we read the papers and see what's happening in the world. At 8.40am we all go off to morning prayers and lessons begin at 9am.

'I suppose our school day is quite long because we don't finish till 4.25pm but after that we can do what we want. We can either watch TV, have dinner or join one of the activity classes such as Keep Fit or Tennis. At 7pm we have to do homework till 9pm. I'm now in the upper sixth so I don't have a set bedtime, but the lower years have to be in bed by certain times. For example, fourth years have to be in bed by 10pm.

'I think that things are quite relaxed here at Cobham. They're strict about some things, like smoking, drinking and seeing boys, but apart from that we are allowed to go out at weekends and a couple of nights a week.

'There's always loads of things to do at school like sport, swimming, weight training etc. I don't even have to wear uniform and can wear jeans to lessons.

'I used to be a day pupil for the first couple of years because my family live so close but now I board as I have much more work to do. Boarding is good fun and I love it. I share with three other girls.'

```
tutorial groups   a set bedtime
strict   good fun
```

Name: Sophie Woodrow
Age: 10
School: The Rudolf Steiner Waldorf School, Bristol
Type: Alternative School

'My school is a bit different from other schools. It's based on the teachings of Rudolf Steiner (a European educational philosopher), and is for children aged between 4 and 14. There's not a big emphasis put on exams at our school because the teachers don't believe in competition, but in cooperation. We do take GCSEs but they're not as important as they would be in state schools.

'It's different in other ways too as in it's funded by parental contributions, and we don't have a headmaster - our teachers make decisions between themselves.

'There's a lot of emphasis on the arts at Steiner schools. We do Eurythmy, which is a sort of music and dance, and music and art. We learn French and German from an early age and even perform plays in foreign languages. We do English three times a week and Maths twice a week. The only thing I don't like about our school is that we aren't taught to read until we're about seven, which I found a bit late. We don't have many trips but we do most sports. We aren't allowed to do football. I think it's to do with not believing in competition.

'School starts at nine o'clock when we have to say a verse. We do this every day - the same verse, although I'm not too sure why we do this. Then we have a lesson with our main teacher for about an hour, then a break and two more lessons. Lunch is half an hour to an hour, after which we have three lessons.

'I like my school because it's so friendly and we don't wear school uniforms, but I don't feel we learn enough here. Once when I visited another school some girls teased us about going to this school. I have thought about going to other schools but it's hard to leave my friends and the teachers, who I like here'.

```
funded   parental contributions
a verse   teased
```

b Discuss any surprises you got while you were reading these texts and any differences between these schools and the one you go/went to.

c Which of the three schools would you most like to go to? Why?

d Do you know any other kinds of 'alternative' schools?

4 Interview two people about the schools they went to, using the headings in **2**, and any others you can think of. Report back in groups.

5 You are going to listen to two 16 year old students, Helen and Nicholas giving their opinion on school issues.

a Look at the extracts from what they say. What do you think they are going to be talking about?

Helen *It does stop people being horrible about other people's clothes.*
What is *it*?
Nicholas *if they grew up with them they'd get to know them.*
What are *they* and *them*?

 b Listen once and see if you were correct.

c What are the main points that they are both making? Do you agree?

6 In groups think of all the arguments for and against the points made by Helen and Nicholas. Appoint a spokesperson to present the arguments to the class.

7 Write a short essay putting the points for and against one of the two issues discussed. Conclude by giving your own opinion.

HOMEWORK

Read the two texts you did not read in class, and do the vocabulary exercise.

UNIT 8 EDUCATION

23 Discussing Lessons

1 Listen to three ten year old boys, Damian (extract 1), Thomas (extract 2) and Dermot (extract 3) talking about what they like and dislike about primary school.

Before you listen:

Can you guess which subjects they will like and dislike?
Can you guess which other things about school they will like and/or dislike?

a   Answer the questions below for each boy.
i   What subjects do they like doing?
ii What subjects don't they like doing?
iii What other things do they dislike?
iv What other things do they like?
v   What do they feel about getting up early?

b   Compare your notes in groups.

2 In pairs, interview each other about your memories of primary school and report back in groups. Ask each other about:

the first day at school
the teachers you liked/disliked
the subjects you liked/disliked
your friends
other?

3 In late 1989 Britain decided to follow the example of most other countries and introduce a National Curriculum into schools. Read the extract below and answer the questions.

THE NATIONAL CURRICULUM

For most of this century primary and secondary schools in England and Wales have been able to determine their own curriculum (albeit under the supervision of one of the 104 Local Education Authorities, the city and county councils responsible for running schools). Teachers and heads, after varying degrees of consultation with their school governors, have been free to decide whether to teach maths on Monday morning or English on Thursday afternoon; which books and teaching methods they will use; how much time to allocate to each activity; and whether to teach academic subjects like history and geography separately, study interdisciplinary topics like 'Our Town', 'Health Education' and 'The Environment' or, more usually, do both.

The arguments for and against a National Curriculum have been well aired during the last few years. Supporters claimed that, since we were one of the few countries in Europe which did not have one, it was about time we came into line; that children who moved schools would simply carry on where they had left off; that teachers would have the security of an agreed structure within which to work; that parents and employers would be able to see what had been covered during schooling; that children would have an entitlement to study a foreign language or science, rather than it being left to the whim of individual schools.

Critics feared that teachers' imagination and commitment would be inhibited if they were told what to teach; that it might be more difficult to relate teaching to children's needs and interests, producing clones rather than individuals; that a government approved curriculum could be the first step towards the teaching of 'State-think'; that a curriculum conceived around single academic subjects might rule out interesting topic and project work, especially in the primary schools, where it was a proud tradition; that planning was being dominated by the requirement for children to be given national tests at the ages of seven, eleven and fourteen and sixteen.

UNIT 8 EDUCATION | LESSON 23

THE SUBJECTS
From the autumn, schools must teach nine subjects to all pupils aged 5-14; three core subjects: English, maths and science; and six foundation subjects: technology and design, history, geography, music, art and physical education, plus a modern foreign language to secondary pupils.

Religious education will have to be offered by all schools. Children will also have time to study subjects outside the National Curriculum such as a second modern foreign language, Latin or the so-called 'technical and vocational educational initiatives'. The main difference between core and foundation subjects is that pupils will spend longer each week on core subjects, about 12 periods for each in secondary schools. Cross curricular and 'theme' work, especially in primary schools, will still be possible.

LEVELS AND TARGETS
All National Curriculum subjects will have Attainment Targets (goals showing what children should know or do) at each stage and Programmes of Study (descriptions of what they should be taught). For music, art and physical education the guidelines will be broader and may not have the statutory backing given to other subjects.

    a According to the article what were the five arguments for and five arguments against a National Curriculum

    b What are 'core' and 'foundation' subjects?

    c What is the difference between them?

4 a Do you think a National Curriculum is a good idea? Why/why not?

    b Discuss the differences between this system and the system in your country.

5 Match the words from the text in **a** to **j** to their equivalents in **i** to **x**

a	curriculum	**i**	stopped
b	interdisciplinary/ cross-curriculum	**ii**	be allowed to
c	came into line	**iii**	a course of study
d	left off	**iv**	concerned with a job
e	have an entitlement	**v**	stop/put an end to
f	whim	**vi**	across different subjects
g	inhibited	**vii**	conform
h	clones	**viii**	restricted
i	rule out	**ix**	parts of the same
j	vocational	**x**	sudden desire

6 Read the following extracts in which Paula and Nicholas talk about teaching in schools. Then answer the questions and discuss what they said with someone else.

Paula
Yes, I think in certain subjects it's important to stream people because the more intelligent are held back by the slower and the slower are intimidated by the people who are brighter. In certain things it's important to mix abilities because it all depends on your opinion in some subjects, not on how bright you are, but in things like maths and probably languages I think it's important to separate them so people can go at their own speed.

   a **i** What word does Paula use to describe separating pupils according to ability?
       ii What word does she use to describe 'intelligent' pupils?
      iii What can happen to these pupils, according to Paula?

   b Do you agree with her?

LESSON 23 — UNIT 8 EDUCATION

Nicholas

I think perhaps we tend to sort of specialise in our subjects too early and I reckon we should carry on doing about, well, the whole curriculum of subjects until we're 18 as they do in, you know, France, because I think you sort of specialise in languages. Perhaps you're good at it but you're just so specialised yet you have no sort of education of anything else and I think this is a bad thing really. They should be sort of generally fully educated by the time you leave school and not just in one particular area.

    c Do you agree with Nicholas? Why/why not?

Paula

I think a lot more subjects could be made more relevant to the world, to the life we live. Languages I think ought to be taught with more emphasis on the oral side. I mean the oral's only a very small part of the exams and we don't often speak the language in our lessons, we just write it. I mean, it's all very well to get it grammatically correct but you've got to be able to speak it if you want to use the language.

    d Why do students not speak foreign languages very much in the classroom?

    e Do you agree that 'being grammatically correct' is not the only important thing in language learning?

    f Do you agree with Paula?

HOMEWORK

Write a short essay discussing the differences between lessons in your country and in Britain. Consider what is taught and how it is taught and how well schooling in your country prepares students for future life and work. Describe the curriculum at schools in your country. How similar is it to the National Curriculum in England and Wales?

UNIT 8 — EDUCATION

24 University Life

1 a Read the text 'A Day in the world of Joann Davies' once quickly. The paragraphs are numbered. Some paragraphs are about one topic, others mention more than one topic.

Which paragraph(s) mention(s):
i the disadvantages of living in self-catering accommodation
ii the problems of living on a student grant
iii working in the laboratory
iv social life at university

A DAY IN THE WORLD OF... JOANN DAVIES, 19, a second-year physics student at Manchester University

1 The sounds of Radio One on my clock-radio wake me and after pressing the snooze button several times, I get up to see if the shower is free. This is rare - one of the drawbacks of sharing a flat with six other girls.

2 By 9 am I'm having coffee and a round of toast before taking a five-minute walk to the laboratories. On the way I collect my mail from Grove House, the amenities building for the 120 flats which comprise Whitworth Park where I live. I love receiving letters from old school friends, but letters from the bank reminding me of my overdraft aren't so welcome. Learning to survive on a grant, even when supplemented by money from holiday jobs, isn't easy and one of the great challenges of university life.

3 There are 175 second-year students studying physics, either on its own or combined with another subject, and I suppose I know about 30 quite well. That's the advantage of being one of only 20 girls in the group - you get known quickly.

4 I have two or three lectures each day. Most are compulsory, but two or three subjects a year may be chosen from a long list of options. Questions may be asked but generally audience participation is minimal.

5 Any problems that do occur can be discussed with a personal tutor at weekly intervals. One day a week is spent in the laboratory. We usually work in pairs spending two or three lab days on one of a wide range of experiments.

6 On a good day lectures run consecutively and are over by lunchtime. Other times there's an hour or two between each one and it's difficult to fill in the spare time constructively. When lectures are over, I go back to the flat, often with friends. Then until about 5pm I attempt one of the problem sheets that are given out in abundance.

7 Once a week a group of us goes shopping, stocking up with supplies from the nearest supermarket (much cheaper than local shops). Walking back heavily laden, I sometimes regret not opting for catered accommodation, I usually cook my main meal at night, or have a takeaway and sometimes there are dinner parties.

8 Between five and six people drop in for a chat and tea. After, there's time to do a couple of hours work or watch television, depending on how strong-willed you feel. Then more friends congregate, either in someone's flat or in Grove House where they have film shows and discos at the weekend and two bars and a games room which open every night. At weekends we often try out Manchester nightlife. The future? I haven't decided what I will do yet, though I may teach or find work in industry. At the moment I'm just looking forward to my next two years at Manchester. We work hard here, but have lots of fun too.

b Read the text more closely and decide if the following statements are true or false.

i Joann gets up as soon as she wakes up.
ii It's sometimes a problem to have a shower.
iii There are a lot of girls studying physics.
iv Lectures usually go on all day.
v Joann enjoys life at university.

LESSON 24 UNIT 8 EDUCATION

2 Find a word or phrase which means the same as:

a sleep for a short time
b disadvantages
c money you owe the bank
d a sum of money, given by the government
e accommodation, with food included

3 You are going to hear two university students in Britain discussing what they like and find difficult about being at university. The first speaker is called Justine and the second is called Beverley. What do you predict they will say?

a Listen, and complete these sentences.

Justine thinks that the best thing is the _____ **i** _____ She has had to take the responsibility of _____ **ii** _____ a house and budgeting her _____ **iii** _____ She found that the best thing was _____ **iv** _____ .

Beverley agrees that _____ **v** _____ is the most important aspect of university life. Having to _____ **vi** _____ and pay the _____ **vii** _____ gives you a strong sense of _____ **viii** _____ and it's a very _____ **ix** _____ thing to do.

Justine says you have to be disciplined about _____ **x** _____ because your _____ **xi** _____ are not there to make you do it.

Beverley agrees that at exam times you have to be careful not to _____ **xii** _____ .

b Is it normal for people to leave home at 18 and go away to university in your country, as it is in Britain? Do you think it is a good idea? Why/why not?

4 Look at these two extracts where two people are talking about the subjects you study at university.

a Take one of the statements and either support or reject it, giving your opinions in groups.

Nicholas
I think the good thing about doing a degree is that once you've done one the fact that you've studied to that kind of level is an indication of your intelligence, and so it doesn't really matter what subject you're doing. Many people accept you on jobs which are completely... have nothing to do with your specialist subject because you have studied to that level.

Roger
The majority of university subjects are very abstract, very academic - useful for your own development but not that useful for future employment - I mean, two thirds of people who go to university in this country do it for liberal arts subjects for their own development.

b What alternatives are there in your country to studying at university, if you want to go on to further education? Which would you prefer and why?

HOMEWORK

Interview someone either from your own country or another one about their experiences at university and write a paragraph entitled 'A Day in the World of...'.

UNIT 9   PETS AND WILDLIFE

25 A 'Good Day Out' at the Zoo?

1 Write down the names of as many zoo animals as you can, and compare with another student. Do you know which countries they come from?

2 Listen to five people giving their opinions on zoos. Tick the box according to whether they like or dislike zoos, or whether they are undecided.

	Like	Dislike	Unsure
Keith			
Judith			
Chris			
Karen			
John			

Listen again and make notes of all the arguments the speakers give for and against zoos. Which arguments do you agree/disagree with?

3 Read the first part of an article about zoos.

ZOOS - are they justified?
by Tess Lemmon

1 The adult male gorilla sits in the corner of a small, glass-fronted room and stares into space. One hand rests on a tyre hanging from the low ceiling, the other flicks at pieces of cardboard scattered across the bare floor.

2 Some people come laughing and joking into the ape house. 'Corr! Look at this one - big, isn't he?' 'Must be King Kong.' 'Look at him just sitting there, lazy old thing.' 'He's looking at you. Bet he'd like you for his dinner!' They move on to the chimps and tap on the glass.

3 One of the main justifications for zoos is meant to be the valuable contribution they make towards education.

4 Zoos often claim that people 'need to see animals in the flesh' before taking an interest in their natural lives and the need to conserve them.

5 But as the above typical situation shows, there are two ways in which the most traditional zoos are failing to carry out their claims about education.

6 The first way is to do with education in its narrowest sense:
What does a zoo teach you about wild animals? What do you learn as you wander from cage to cage?
That gorillas live alone in small rooms and flick cardboard? Or that polar bears live in concrete pits and sway from side to side all day?

7 Gorillas are very sociable, peaceful animals, living in well-ordered groups consisting of an adult male plus several females and their offspring. They live in the dense forests of Africa and feed on a variety of vegetation.

8 Polar bears are often solitary, wandering across the ice and snow of the Arctic, feeding on seals, fish and birds. Bears are extremely inquisitive, intelligent animals.

9 For many people zoos have always been here so they are the expected and accepted method of keeping exotic animals in captivity.

10 Those people laughing at the gorilla have gone to the zoo for a good time. They keep cats and dogs and hate the thought of cruelty to animals. Indeed, every morning on her way to work one of the women in the group used to pass a garden where a dog was up in a small crate. It barked and barked.

UNIT 9 PETS AND WILDLIFE   LESSON 25

She found this situation totally unacceptable and reported it the RSPCA. But she happily goes to the zoo and accepts conditions which are just as bad as those of the dog.
Many zoo people say that nothing substitutes actually getting close to a live elephant, lion, gorilla. And they say this is particularly important for young people. But what kind of close encounter is this?
And what price are the animals paying so that this 'nation of animal-lovers' can go and look at them whenever the fancy takes us?
11 And what sort of human beings are we if we find it fun to run from cage to cage poking and joking?

There are alternatives. As far as education is concerned, TV nature programmes teach us far more than zoos about how animals live in the wild, where they belong. There are also exciting ways modern technology can help us to enjoy and understand animals - stuffed animals in museums are being replaced by lifelike models of animals and their habitat, and also by clever uses of videos, films, slides and sound.
   Many zoos talk about conservation, but often they are only just talking about it. Even if they do breed rare animals there are very many problems involved in returning them to the wild.
   Wouldn't the money and expert knowledge be better spent in conserving animals in the wild? This would not only be better for the animals, it would be better for us - we might begin to understand that human beings share the earth with many thousands of other species who have just as much right to live their own lives as we have.

a What is the main justification given for having zoos, according to the the writer? Are the following statements true or false, according to the article?

i Zoos are supposed to be necessary because they teach people about animals.
ii Zoos keep animals in the same conditions that they are used to having in the wild.
iii The writer thinks animals are often bored and unhappy in the zoo.
iv Only people who are cruel to animals go to the zoo.
v The writer thinks it is cruel to go and stare at the animals.

b Do you agree with the writer? Can you give any more examples from your own experience of animals who are clearly unhappy in zoos?

c Read the next part of the article.

i What other suggestions are made about educating the public about wildlife? Do you agree?
ii Does the writer think most zoos are helping to conserve rare animals?
iii What is her recommendation? Do you agree?

4 Look at the first extract again and express the following words and expressions from the article in your own words:

a stares into space (para 1)
b is meant to be (para 3)
c in the flesh (para 4)
d offspring (para 7)
e solitary (para 8)

HOMEWORK

Zoos perform a useful function in society.

Ask a few people about their views on zoos and write a short summary of their reactions in the form of a survey.

UNIT 9 PETS AND WILDLIFE

26 A Strange Obsession?

ANIMAL CRAZY

POLICE blocked off a section of motorway to help a frightened swan become airborne. They spotted the swan struggling to take off by the side of the M2, near Rochester, Kent. But turbulence from fast moving traffic was making it impossible for the bird. So the kindly cops coned off the hard shoulder and slow lane. Traffic slowed to a crawl in a tailback, and the swan took off on a clear runway.
It's amazing the trouble people will go to for animals . . .

- A £27,000,000 bypass at Rathno, West Lothian, was held up when animal lovers protested it would destroy a colony of rare great crested newts, now tunnels have been built under the road linking the newts' breeding and feeding grounds.

- When pensioner John Yeates, of Worcester, saw a hedgehog floating upside down in his fishpond he fished it out and revived it with the kiss of life.

- At Meriden, Warwicks, a duck-lover risked arrest by 'stealing' 250,000 gallons of water to fill a dried-up village pond - for the ducks to splash around in during drought restrictions. He connected a pump to the fire hydrant and used warning cones and a flashing light to look official.

- Millionaire Maurice Oberstein, boss of Polygram records, paid £1,500 for a whole page 'happy birthday' advertisement to his red setter Charlie, in Music Week. He donated £1,500 to Battersea Dogs Home.

1 a Look at the magazine extract above and complete the summary below.

Police blocked the hard shoulder and the _____ **i** _____ of a motorway so that a swan could _____ **ii** _____ .
_____ **iii** _____ had to be built in order to protect a colony of _____ **iv** _____ when a new _____ **v** _____ was being built and animal lovers _____ **vi** _____ .
A _____ **vii** _____ was given the _____ **viii** _____ when a man saw it _____ **ix** _____ in his pond.
A man stole _____ **x** _____ to fill a pond for _____ **xi** _____ to live in during the _____ **xii** _____ restrictions.
A millionaire paid £1,500 for an _____ **xiii** _____ in a music magazine to celebrate his dog's _____ **xiv** _____ .

b What is your opinion of this sort of behaviour? Is it only a British obsession, or do people in your country do eccentric things where animals or pets are concerned? Can you think of any examples?

2 1  2

3

a Sometimes people can remind you of animals. If the people above were animals what sort do you think they would be and why? Discuss in groups.
b Listen to three people describing an animal and match the description to one of the pictures above.
c Think of somebody in the class and say what they would be if they were an animal. The others must guess who it is.

3 The RSPCA is a society which protects animals (Royal Society for the Prevention of Cruelty to Animals). In this particular week he had to do all the following things. Number them in the order he had to do them.

a Read the diary of the RSPCA Inspector opposite.
i   rescue a cat from a tree
ii inspect a cattle market
iii rescue an owl
iv rescue a hedgehog
v   rescue a horse
vi rescue a swan
vii investigate a monkey in a garden
viii investigate a badly treated dog
ix investigate an abandoned tarantula

Dear Diary
AN RSPCA INSPECTOR

MONDAY
Woke up about sevenish, had a wash, made some breakfast, and got into my uniform. I work from home for about an hour before going to our main headquarters, so the calls started coming through at about nine. Most of them were from people looking for advice and that sort of thing.

At 9.30 I transferred all my home calls to the RSPCA headquarters, and then made my way there. The first call I got there was from a woman who could hear a fluttering noise from her chimney stack. I went round and the lady said she didn't mind me making a mess of her fireplace, so I pulled it to bits and saw a barn owl flapping around. He was a bit damaged but the vet fixed him up.

After lunch I followed up a complaint from someone who thought a dog living near to them was being mistreated, so I visited the own and found her lovely dog confined in a tiny outside toilet. When I confronted the owner, she said the dog wasn't housetrained so it was locked up outside. I gave the woman some advice about how to house-train and the like. Then grabbed a sandwich for lunch, followed up a few routine enquiries and made my way home.

I had to do night-duty tonight, so I was sitting at the phone at about six. Got a call from someone who thought that a neighbour had abandoned two dogs, a cat and a tarantula spider. Went round that evening and saw the animals through the window. No-one seemed to be at home, so I fed the animals through the letterbox and put crushed ice through as well, so that they could be watered. Took a few statements from the neighbours and went home.

TUESDAY
First thing this morning I got some paperwork out of the way and then drove into the office. First call of the day was to check a hedgehog which had been trapped in a drain. It was fine, so I released it - a nice happy ending.

Got a call at the office telling me that a horse was trapped in a barbed wire fence. I arrived at the scene about 10 minutes later and the horse had already collapsed. I cut the barbed wire from the horse, and then the vet arrived. The horse was in a bad way when the vet took it away. I just hope it pulls through.

Went to rescue a cat from a tree - it'd been up there for a couple of days. In cases like these it's better to leave it up there for a while so that it learns a lesson. So many times I've rescued cats from trees and once I've brought them down they run back up again.

Went back to the house where the animals were abandoned and still no-one was there, so the police and I broke down the door. Thankfully the tarantula was in a glass cage, which I was glad about. Didn't relish the thought of manhandling one of them.

UNIT 9 PETS AND WILDLIFE — LESSON 26

WEDNESDAY

Went to a cattle market and witness the unloading of the sheep to check there was no overcrowding, and had a look at the animals. One cow was extremely lame so I separated it from the others. Also had a gossip with the locals. It's good to be friendly with them because they can be really helpful at times.

In the afternoon I got a call from a neighbour of the people who'd abandoned their pets at home. Went round to their house to confront them - not a though which I relished. They did go a bit crazy at first, but when they calmed down I asked them why they'd left the animals to care for themselves for nearly four days. They made some feeble excuse about having an argument, so I interviewed them under caution, and told them they'd probably be charged.

Had this evening off, so I went down to the beach to do some windsurfing. I'm a member of our local club and tonight we had a competition with the local navy team. We won!

THURSDAY

Emergency call this morning about a swan roaming about on a motorway. Arrived at the scene to find 10 police officers chasing it. We stopped all the traffic and tried to catch it - with people in cars giving us really strange looks. Managed to catch the swan and took it to the rescue home.

Someone called to say that they thought a neighbour's dog wasn't being cared for too well. When I arrived at the house, an 81-year old lady answered the door. The dog was quite poorly but it was pretty old and they only thing the old lady had in the world. I decided it wouldn't be good to take it away from her, so I told her I'd call every so often to see how she and the dog were doing. Quite sad.

Watched the telly most of the night, and then forced myself to do some housework. Not the highlight of the day.

FRIDAY

First day off for ages. Met a couple of friends this morning for a game of squash, which I won, so I had to foot the bill for the lunches. Wish I'd lost! Then went back to the beach for more windsurfing. It doesn't exactly relax me, but I do enjoy it.

Had to be back home by six because I was back on night duty this evening. My girlfriend came over for dinner, but the phone went every five minutes so it wasn't terribly romantic. Still, she raved about my dinner. I must admit I'm a pretty good cook.

Highlight of the evening was when I got a call from someone who said there was a monkey loose in their back garden. I thought they were pulling my leg but it turned out to be true.

---

b Give more information about what happened to the animals. Work in groups and try not to look back at the text.

i What was fluttering and flapping, and where?
ii What was locked in an outside toilet, and why?
iii What animals were reported as abandoned?
iv What was trapped in a drain?
v What was trapped in a fence?
vi What was stuck up a tree?
vii What couldn't walk?
viii What was on the motorway?
ix What was old and ill?
x What was found in a back garden?

4 Explain the following words and expressions in your own words;

a made my way there (Monday)
b fixed him up (Monday)
c in a bad way (Tuesday)
d pulls through (Tuesday)
e broke down (Tuesday)
f witnessed the unloading (Wednesday)
g gossip (Wednesday)
h calmed down (Wednesday)
i feeble (Wednesday)
j charged (Wednesday)
k roaming (Thursday)
l poorly (Thursday)
m highlight (Thursday)
n raved (Friday)
o pulling my leg (Friday)

HOMEWORK

Write a week in the life of your life, in the form of a diary. Refer back to the RSPCA diary and notice that you don't always have to include personal pronouns when you are writing a diary: *Woke up about sevenish, had a wash...*

UNIT 9 PETS AND WILDLIFE

27 The Animals We Might Lose Forever

1 *I've been involved in the Green Party for three years. I don't have any fear for myself for the Nineties, but I have for the planet. What gives man the right to slaughter whales? They think that 50 years ago there were 40,000 tigers in the East and now there's only 8,000 to 10,000: such fantastic creatures. I hope these animals are saved in the Nineties. The elephant could be extinct by the end of the decade if they carry on.*

This is one man's worry about the future. Do you know of any animals that are threatened by man? Why? What is being done about it?

2 What are the names of the animals in the pictures? Do you know where they come from and why they face extinction?

1   Disaster did not strike the tiger until a post-war demand for hardwood triggered a massive onslaught on tropical forests. Vast areas, which had stood for 60 million years, disappeared at the rate of 50 acres a minute. Deprived of shelter and prey, the tiger was doomed. In 1972, its population had dropped from 40,000 to less than 2,000 in 40 years. It's now doubled on WWF reserves.

2   The blue whale, the largest animal ever to have lived on earth - reaching lengths of 100 feet and weighing up to 150 tons. The whale was exploited as a source of meat, fats and oils. Its food-sieving plates (baleen) were used to make whalebone corsets. Despite repeated warnings from scientists, whalers continued to kill blue whales until their number was one thirtieth of its original level.

3   Wild black rhinos have become the ultimate symbol of threatened African wildlife. Thirty years ago there were more than 100,000 of them. Today there are probably fewer than 4,000. In Kenya, Zambia and Zimbabwe, poaching rhino horn is still the way to a fortune.

UNIT 9 PETS AND WILDLIFE — LESSON 27

4 There used to be 300 species of elephant - today there are just the African and Indian. In Africa, where an estimated 75,000 still survive, 10,000 a year are shot by poachers for their tusks. The trade has a street value of $1 billion. Herds return to the best places to find crops and gardens and are killed by farmers.

5 Emblem of the World Wildlife Fund, the giant panda faced extinction by the end of the century until, ironically, man stepped in. For it was man's destruction of the forest which had left the pandas in small, isolated pockets. Leopards occasionally kill the younger ones, and pandas can be accidentally snared in the traps set to snare musk deer. Occasionally giant pandas are shot: their skins are prized as trophies, or used as rugs and wall hangings.

Find out the following information as quickly as you can, by looking through the texts above.

a What first started the disappearance of tigers, and why?
b When did this happen?
c Which animal reaches 100 feet in length?
d Why was the blue whale hunted?
e In which countries is rhino horn taken illegally?
f Are black or white rhinos in more danger?
g What part of the elephants does ivory come from?
h Which kind of elephant is most at risk?
i How many species of elephant did there use to be?
j Why are giant pandas shot?
k What is being done to save them?

3 Complete the gaps in this word puzzle with words from the text which match the definitions given (the paragraph number is given). If you complete it correctly you will make a word connected to the topic to fit in the box (it begins with e).

1 used (unfairly) for profit (para 2)
2 caught in a trap (para 5)
3 very big (para 1)
4 a group of animals of the same kind that can breed together (para 4)
5 in danger (para 3)
6 plants produced by farmers (para 4)
7 less in quantity (para 3)
8 sure to die (para 1)
9 an animal that is hunted and eaten by other animals (para 1)
10 fierce attack (para 1)
11 no longer in existence (para 5)
12 buying and selling of goods (para 4)
13 killing on a big scale (para 2)

1 e x p l o i t e d
2 . s . . . .
3 . . . s .
4 . . e . .
5 . t . . . . .
6 . r . . .
7 . . . d . .
8 d . . . . .
9 . . y .
10 . . . a . . .
11 . . . . i .
12 . . d .
13 . . . . . t .

HOMEWORK

My Fears For The Future

Write a short paragraph along the lines of the extract at the beginning of the lesson, about your worries for the future. Which world issues worry you most and why?

UNIT 10 BRIBERY AND CORRUPTION

28 Bribery...

1 Read the first part of this story by Ruth Rendell and answer the questions that follow.

BRIBERY AND CORRUPTION

Everyone who makes a habit of dining out in London knows that Potters in Marylebone High Street is one of the most expensive of eating places, Nicholas Hawthorne, who usually dined in his rented room or in a steak house, was deceived by the humble-sounding name. When Annabel said, 'Let's go to Potters,' he agreed quite happily.

It was the first time he had taken her out. She was a small girl with very little to say for herself. In her little face her eyes looked huge and appealing - a flying fox face, Nicholas thought. She suggested they take a taxi to Potters 'because it's difficult to find'. Seeing that it was the High Street, Nicholas didn't think it would have been more difficult to find on foot than in a taxi but he said nothing.

He was already wondering what this meal was going to cost. Potters was a grand and imposing restaurant. The windows were of that very clear but slightly warped glass that bespeaks age, and the doors of a dark red wood that looked as if it had been polished every day for fifty years. Because the curtains were drawn and the interior not visible, it appeared as if they were approaching some private residence, perhaps a rich man's town house.

Immediately inside the doors was a bar where three couples sat about in black leather chairs. A waiter took Annabel's coat and they were conducted to a table in the restaurant. Nicholas, though young, was perceptive. He had expected Annabel to be made as shy and awkward by this place as he was himself but she seemed to have shed her diffidence with her coat. And when waiters approached with menus and the wine list she said boldly that she would start with a Pernod.

What was it all going to cost? Nicholas looked unhappily at the prices and was thankful he had his newly acquired credit card with him. Live now, pay later - but, oh God, he would still have to pay.

a Is Nicholas rich? How do you know?
b What kind of restaurant is Potters?
c What kind of relationship did Nicholas and Annabel have?
d How did Nicholas feel in the restaurant?
e How did Annabel feel about it?

UNIT 10 BRIBERY AND CORRUPTION — LESSON 28

2 Read the next part of the story and answer the questions that follow.

> Annabel chose asparagus for her first course and roast grouse for her second. The grouse was the most expensive item on the menu. Nicholas selected vegetable soup and a pork chop. He asked her if she would like red or white wine and she said one bottle wouldn't be enough, would it, so why not have one of each?
>
> She didn't speak at all while they ate. He remembered reading in some poem or other how the poet marvelled of a schoolmaster that one small head could carry all he knew. Nicholas wondered how one small body could carry all Annabel ate. She devoured roast potatoes with her grouse and red cabbage and runner beans, and when she heard the waiter recommending braised artichokes to the people at the next table she said she would have some of those too. He prayed she wouldn't want another course. But that fawning insinuating waiter had to come up with the sweet trolley.
>
> 'We have fresh strawberries, madam.'
> 'In November?' said Annabel, breaking her silence.
> 'How lovely.'
> Naturally she would have them. Drinking the dregs of his wine, Nicholas watched her eat the strawberries and cream and then call for a slice of chocolate roulade. He ordered coffee. Did sir and madam wish for a liqueur? Nicholas shook his head vehemently. Annabel said she would have a green chartreuse. Nicholas know knew that this was of all liqueurs the pearl - and necessarily the most expensive.

   a What did Annabel order for her meal?
   b What did Nicholas order?
   c What was the most expensive item of food on the menu?

3 In groups of three, act out the dialogue between Annabel, Nicholas and the waiter. Begin with the waiter coming to take the order. The waiter should try to encourage Annabel to choose what she wants. Nicholas should try to persuade her not to eat and so much, and choose less expensive dishes.

4 Read the next part of the story and complete the gaps in the summary.

> By now he was so frightened about the bill and so repelled by her concentrated guzzling that he needed briefly to get away from her. It was plain she had come out with him only to stuff and drink herself into a stupor. He excused himself and went off in the direction of the men's room.
>
> In order to reach it he had to pass across one end of the bar. The place was still half-empty but during the past hour - it was now nine o'clock - another couple had come in and were sitting at a table in the centre of the floor. The man was middle-aged with thick silver hair and a lightly tanned taut-skinned face. His right arm was round the shoulder of his companion, a very young, very pretty blonde girl, and he was whispering something in her ear. Nicholas recognized him at once as the chairman of the company for which his own father had been sales manager until two years before when he had been made redundant on some specious pretext. The company was called Sorensen-McGill and the silver-haired man was Julius Sorensen.
>
> With all the fervour of a young man loyal to a beloved parent, Nicholas hated him. But Nicholas was a very young man and it was beyond his strength to cut Sorensen. He muttered a stiff good evening and plunged for the men's room where he turned out his pockets, counted the notes in his wallet and tried to calculate what he already

owed to the credit card company. If necessary he would have to borrow from his father, though he would hate to do that, knowing as he did that his father had been living on a reduced income even since that beast Sorensen fired him. Borrow from his father, try and put off paying the rent for a month if he could, cut down on his smoking, maybe give up altogether . . .

When he came out, feeling almost sick, Sorensen and the girl had moved father apart from each other. They didn't look at him and Nicholas too looked the other way.

While he was going to the men's room Nicholas saw a _____ **a** _____ who he recognised as the _____ **b** _____ of the company his _____ **c** _____ had worked for until he had been made _____ **d** _____ . The man's name was _____ **e** _____ . Although Nicholas _____ **f** _____ him he _____ **g** _____ him before he went in the men's room. There he _____ **h** _____ what he _____ **i** _____ the credit card company.

5 Read the next part of the story.

Annabel was on her second green chartreuse and gobbling up petit fours. He had thought her face was like that of a flying fox and now he remembered that flying fox is only a pretty name for a fruit bat. Eating a marzipan orange, she looked just like a rapacious little fruit bat. And she was very drunk.

'I feel ever so sleepy and strange,' she said. 'Maybe I've got one of those viruses. Could you pay the bill?'

It took Nicholas a long time to catch the waiter's eye. When he did the man merely homed in on them with the coffee pot. Nicholas surprised himself with his own firmness.

'I'd like the bill,' he said in the tone of one who declares to higher authority that he who is about to die salutes thee.

In half a minute the waiter was back. Would Nicholas be so good as to come with him and speak to the maitre d'hotel? Nicholas nodded, dumbfounded. What had happened? What had he done wrong? Annabel was slouching back in her chair, her big eyes half-closed, a trickle of something orange dribbling out of the corner of her mouth. They were going to tell him to remove her, that she had disgraced the place, not to come here again. He followed the waiter, his hands clenched.

A huge man spoke to him, a man with the beak and plumage of a king penguin. 'Your bill has been paid, sir.'

Nicholas stared. 'I don't know what you mean.'
'Your father paid it, sir. Those were my instructions, to tell you your father had settled your bill.'

The relief was tremendous. He seemed to grow tall again and light and free. It was as if someone had made him a present of - well, what would it have been? Sixty pounds? Seventy? And he understood at once.

Are the following statements true or false? Discuss your answers in groups.
a Nicholas had changed his opinion of Annabel.
b Annabel was ill.
c Nicholas thought the restaurant were going to complain about Annabel.
d Nicholas had to go and speak to a penguin.
e His father had paid the bill.

UNIT 10 BRIBERY AND CORRUPTION   LESSON 28

6 Guess what has happened in groups. Then read the text and see if your guess is correct.

> Sorensen had paid his bill and said he was his father. It was a little bit of compensation for what Sorensen had done in dismissing his father. He had paid out sixty pounds to show me he meant well, to show that he wanted, in a small way, to make up for injustice.
>
> Tall and free and masterful, Nicholas said, 'Call me a cab, please,' and then he went and shook Annabel awake in quite a lordly way.
>
> His euphoria lasted for nearly an hour, long after he had pushed the somnolent Annabel through her own front door, then climbed the stairs up to the furnished room he rented and settled down to the crossword in the evening paper.

7 Look at the dictionary entries below and then read the next part of the story.

> **bribe** /v 1 [T1 (*with* or *into*);V3] to influence unfairly (esp. someone in a position of trust) by favours or gifts: *He bribed the policeman (to let him go free/into letting him go free).* (fig.) *The child was being bribed with a piece of cake to go to bed quietly.* 2 [X9] to get or make in this way: *He bribed himself/his way onto the committee.*
>
> **cor-rupt** /1 [T1:10] to make morally bad: cause to change from good to bad: *Complete power corrupts completely.* 2 [T1] to influence (a person. esp. a public official) improperly: BRIBE: *He was sent to prison for trying to corrupt a policeman with money.* 3 [Wv5:T1] to change the original form of (a language, set of teachings, etc) in a bad way: *Has English been corrupted or made richer by the introduction of foreign words?* - ~ible adj - ~ibility/   /n [U].

> Things would have turned out very differently if he hadn't started that crossword. 'Twelve across: Bone in mixed byre goes with corruption. (7 letters)' Then I and the Y were already in. He got the answer after a few seconds - 'Bribery'. 'Rib' in an anagram of 'byre'. 'Bribery'.
>
> He laid down the paper and looked at the opposite wall. That which goes with corruption. How could he ever have been such a fool, such a naive innocent fool, as to suppose a man like Sorensen cared about injustice or ever gave a thought to wrongful dismissal or even believed for a moment he could have been wrong? Of course Sorensen hadn't been trying to make restitution, of course he hadn't paid the bill out of kindness and remorse. He had paid it as a bribe.

a Why was Nicholas so upset by the clue 'bribery'?
b Why do you think Nicholas suspects Sorensen of bribing him?
c What do you think will happen next?

HOMEWORK

Imagine Nicholas didn't have his bill paid by Sorensen and didn't have enough money (his credit card company refused to let him exceed his limit). Write the dialogue between Nicholas and the waiter, based on this situation.

UNIT 10 BRIBERY AND CORRUPTION

29 ...and Corruption

1 Read the next part of the story.

> He had paid the bribe to shut Nicholas's mouth because he didn't want anyone to know he had been out drinking with a girl, embracing a girl, who wasn't his wife. It was bribery, the bribery that went with corruption.
>
> Once, about three years before, Nicholas had been with his parents to a party Sorensen had given for his staff and Mrs Sorensen had been the hostess. A brown-haired mousey little woman, he remembered her, and all of forty-five which seemed like old age to Nicholas. Sorensen had paid that bill because he didn't want his wife to find out he had a girlfriend young enough to be his daughter.
>
> He had bought him, Nicholas thought, bribed and corrupted him - or tried to. Because he wasn't going to succeed. He needn't think he could kick the Hawthorne family around any more. Once was enough.
>
> It had been nice thinking that he hadn't after all wasted more than half a week's wages on that horrible girl but honour was more important. Honour, surely, meant sacrificing material thing for a principle. Nicholas had a bad night because he kept waking up and thinking of all the material things he would have to go short of during the next few weeks on account of his honour. Nevertheless, by the morning his resolve was fixed. Making sure he had his cheque book with him, he went off to work.

a Did you guess correctly about why Nicholas thought Sorensen was bribing him?
b What do you think 'mousey' means?
c What does Nicholas mean when he says *He needn't think he could kick the Hawthorne family around any more. Once was enough*?
d What do you think Nicholas is going to do next?
e What do you think will happen?

2 Read the next part of the story.

> Several hours passed before he could get the courage together to phone Sorensen-McGill. What was he going to do if Sorensen refused to see him? If only he had a nice fat bank account with five hundred pounds in it he could make the grand gesture and send Sorensen a blank cheque accompanied by a curt and contemptuous letter.
>
> The telephonist who used to answer in the days when he sometimes phoned his father at work answered now. 'Sorensen-McGill. Can I help you?'
>
> His voice rather hoarse, Nicholas asked if he could have an appointment with Mr Sorensen that day on a matter of urgency. He was put though to Sorensen's secretary. There was a delay. Bells rang and switches clicked. The girl came back to the phone and Nicholas was sure she was going to say no.
>
> 'Mr Sorensen asks if one o'clock will suit you?'
>
> In his lunch hour? Of course it would. But what on earth could have induced Sorensen to have sacrificed one of those fat expense account lunches just to see him? Nicholas set off for Berkeley Square, wondering what had made the man so forthcoming. A weak hopeful little voice inside him began once again putting up those arguments which on the previous

UNIT 10 BRIBERY AND CORRUPTION   LESSON 29

evening the voice of a common sense had so decisively refuted.

Perhaps Sorensen really meant well and when Nicholas got there would tell him the paying of the bill has been no bribery but a way of making a present to the son of a once-valued employee. The pretty girl could have been Sorensen's daughter. Nicholas had no idea if the man had children. It was possible he had a daughter. No corruption then, no betrayal of his honour, no need to give up cigarettes or abase himself before his landlord.

They knew him at Sorensen-McGill. He had been there with his father and, besides, he looked like his father. The pretty blond girl hadn't looked in the least like Sorensen. A secretary showed him into the chairman's office. Sorensen was sitting in a yellow leather chair behind a rosewood desk with an inlaid yellow leather top. There were Modigliani-like murals on the wall behind him and on the desk a dark green jade ashtray, stacked with stubs, which the secretary replaced with a clean one of pale green jade.

'Hallo, Nicholas,' said Sorensen. He didn't smile. 'Sit down.'

The only other chair in the room was one of those hi-tech low-slung affairs made of leather hung on a metal frame. Beside it was a black glass coffee table with a black leather padded rim and on the glass lay a magazine open at the centrefold of a nude girl. There are some people who know how to put others at their ease and there are those who know how to put others in difficulties. Nicholas sat down, right down - about three inches from the floor.

a What would Nicholas do if he had enough money?
b What did Nicholas consider, after he had made the appointment?
c Why did he want to believe this?
d What kind of office did Sorensen have?
e What do you think Nicholas's reaction to the office was?

3 Imagine what happens next between Sorensen and Nicholas. Act out the dialogue and decide which student's guess is the most likely.

4
a Listen to the next part of the story and cross out the incorrect statements in the text below.

The girl Sorensen was with was a regular girlfriend of his, who his wife doesn't know about. He is afraid of her finding out and offers to pay Nicholas more money if he will keep his mouth shut. He accuses Nicholas of coming to blackmail him. Nicholas was cold with anger and unemotional. Sorensen was powerful and seemed amused. Nicholas said that he could not be bought in this way. He wrote Sorensen out a cheque for £57 and said that he refused to keep Sorensen's secret. Sorensen put the cheque in his pocket and told Nicholas to leave.

b Try to correct the statements in groups.

5 Listen again and answer the questions.

a Why does Sorensen say *I should have expected this*?
b How does he say his wife would feel?
c What sort of illness does she suffer from?

6 The story has not yet finished. Two mornings later this headline appeared in the paper:

Woman Found Dead in Forest. Murder of Tycoon's Wife.

The woman was Sorensen's wife. In groups, discuss how the story ends.

HOMEWORK

Write a brief summary of what you think happens next based on your discussion in groups. Do not look at the next lesson yet. You can read out your stories in the next class.

UNIT 10 — BRIBERY AND CORRUPTION

30 Revenge!

1 Read out your group's story to the rest of the class. Which ending do you think is most likely?

2 Read the next part of the story

1. Nicholas got out. He walked out of the building with his head in the air. He was still considering sending Sorensen another cheque when, two mornings later, reading his paper in the train, his eye caught the hated name. At first he didn't think the story referred to 'his' Sorensen - and then he knew it did. The headline read: 'Woman Found Dead in Forest. Murder of Tycoon's Wife'.

2. 'The body of a woman,' ran the story beneath, 'was found last night in an abandoned car in Hatfield Forest in Hertfordshire. She had been strangled. The woman was today identified as Mrs Winifred Sorensen, 45, of Eaton Place, Belgravia. She was the wife of Julius Sorensen, chairman of Sorensen-McGill, manufacturers of office equipment.

3. 'Mrs Sorensen had been staying with her mother, Mrs Mary Clifford, at Mrs Clifford's home in Much Hadham. Mrs Clifford said, 'My daughter had intended to stay with me for a further two days. I was surprised when she said she would drive home to London on Tuesday evening.'

4. 'I was not expecting my wife home on Tuesday,' said Mr Sorensen. 'I had no idea she had left her mother's house until I phoned there yesterday. When I realised she was missing I immediately informed the police.'

5. Police are treating the case as murder. That poor woman, thought Nicholas. While she had been driving home to her husband, longing for him probably, needing his company and his comfort, he had been philandering with a girl he had picked up, a girl whose surname he didn't even know. He must now be overcome with remorse. Nicholas hoped it was biting agonized remorse. The contrast was what was so shocking, Sorensen cheek to cheek with a girl, drinking with her, no doubt later sleeping with her; his wife alone, struggling with an attacker in a lonely place in the dark.

6. Nicholas, of course, wouldn't have been surprised if Sorensen had done it himself. Nothing Sorensen could do would have surprised him. The man was capable of any iniquity. Only this he couldn't have done, which none know better than Nicholas. So it was a bit of a shock to be accosted by two policemen when he arrived home that evening. They were waiting in a car outside his gate and they got out as he approached.

7. 'Nothing to worry about, Mr Hawthorne,' said the older of them who introduced himself as a Detective Inspector. 'Just a matter of routine. Perhaps you read about the death of Mrs Winifred Sorensen in your paper today?'
'Yes'
'May we come in?'

8. They followed him upstairs. What could they want of him? Nicholas sometimes read detective stories and it occurred to him that, knowing perhaps of his tenuous connection with Sorensen-McGill, they would want to ask him questions about Sorensen's character and domestic life. In that case they had come to the right witness.

9. He could tell them all right. He could tell them why poor Mrs Sorensen, jealous and suspicious as she must have been, had taken it into her head to leave her mother's house two days early and drive home. Because she had intended to catch her husband in the act. And she would have caught him, found him absent or maybe entertaining that girl in their home, only she had never got home. Some maniac had hitched a lift from her first. Oh yes, he'd tell them! In his room they sat down. They had to sit on the bed for there was only one chair.

UNIT 10 BRIBERY AND CORRUPTION — LESSON 30

Are the following statements true or false according to the text?

a Sorensen's wife had been shot.
b She had been on her way to her mother's house.
c Sorensen thought she was driving home to London that night.
d Nicholas suspected Sorensen of the murder.
e Nicholas went to see the police.
f The police told him Mrs Sorensen must have given someone a lift.

3 Find words or expressions in the text that are similar in meaning to the following:

a thinking about (para 1)
b rich businessman (para 2)
c terribly guilty (para 5)
d wickedness/bad thing (para 6)
e somebody who gives evidence (para 8)

4 Listen to the first part of the listening text and complete the sentences below.

a Mrs Sorensen was killed _____.
b Mr Sorensen had told them _____.
c Nicholas felt very _____.
d The police knew _____.
e They asked Nicholas _____.

5 Listen to the second part of the listening text and answer the following questions:

a Why did Nicholas blush?
b Why do the police think Nicholas is uneasy?
c What is the problem with Mr Sorensen's alibi?
d What is the last question the police ask Nicholas?
e What is his answer?

6 In pairs, imagine one of you is Sorensen and one of you is a policeman. The policeman has gone to arrest Sorensen after the meeting with Nicholas. What do you think they said? Invent the dialogue.

7 Sorensen was sentenced to life imprisonment. How do you think Nicholas felt?

HOMEWORK

Imagine you are writing a report for a 'popular' (less serious) newspaper. Report what Sorensen said he did on the night of the murder.

Teacher's Notes

UNIT 1 MURDER!

The following notes are to help teachers prepare the activities, and provide some further suggestions.

This unit is based on a Roald Dahl short story, *Lamb to the Slaughter*. Begin by asking students if they have read any of Dahl's stories, and telling them that many of his stories (for adults) involve a kind of 'black humour'. The main reading and listening sub-skills (gist, specific information, interpretation and vocabulary deduction) are practised in this unit, and there is plenty of stimulus for oral fluency and writing as well as vocabulary extension. It also provides lots of opportunity for revision of narrative forms.

LESSON 1
'I've got something to tell you.'

Ask students to read the first extract in **1** once quickly before looking at the questions for discussion. Encourage them to back up their answers with evidence from the text, both in this activity and the listening one (in **3**). An alternative to **4** is to ask students to act out the dialogue in pairs. Make it clear in **6** that the story 'jumps' at this stage. Try to encourage them to predict what happened. This is a good opportunity to practise modal forms such as *she may have ..., they could have ...* . The homework could be done orally as groupwork in class first, if there is time.

LESSON 2
'Don't make supper for me. I'm going out.'

As a warmer, encourage students to discuss their stories in groups first and tell the best one to the rest of the class. Make sure students realise where the next part of the story (in **2**) continues from. **4** provides a set of cues for students to recall the story but is also useful revision of regular and irregular past forms. It should be done as a brainstorm, without looking back at the text and could be followed up, if there is time, with work on the different pronunciations of past endings (rapt/liftid/kaerid) and also spelling rules (double consonants). **5** could be followed up with recall of the story, using time linkers and narrative forms (first, after this, when she'd done that ...) in **6** refer students back to this part of the story in Lesson 1. in **7** extra work could be done here on note-taking, and the elaboration of notes into a report (see homework).

LESSON 3
'Get the weapon and you've got the man.'

In **2** an alternative activity would be for students to write out the dialogue and then act it out in front of the class. The vocabulary extension activity in **5** could be followed up by eliciting words connected to murder (strangle, stab, etc.) it also lends itself to sentences such as *it is used for ....ing people with*. Further discussion and 'creative' activities could come in here, for example; a discussion of 'crimes of passion' and the penalties for this. Or a debate on crimes and punishment in general, a discussion of the title, and the two meanings of *Lamb to the Slaughter*, a discussion of how the story could be filmed, and who the best actors/actresses would be for the various parts.

UNIT 2 HEALTH AND FITNESS

This unit focuses on food and fitness, and the vocabulary associated with it. There is plenty of scope in this unit for revision of the language of quantity (*a lot, not much, not enough, some, any,* etc.) the present simple and adverbs of frequency to talk about habit, giving advice, and also question forms.

LESSON 4
You Are What You Eat

The vocabulary activity in **1** is a warmer, where students can brainstorm the vocabulary of food in pairs or groups (it could extend into revision of countable and uncountable nouns). Encourage them to use dictionaries where necessary. This activity should lead naturally into a discussion of what food is good/bad for you and why (in **2**), although some of the vocabulary (*protein*, etc. may need explaining). The quiz, in **4**, and the interview, in **6**, lend themselves well to revision of adverbs of frequency/time expressions and the present simple. **6b** could also lead to revision of ways of giving advice (*you should, if I were you, you'd better*). This is useful input to the letter in Lesson **5**. Practice in direct and indirect questions is given in **7**, and the teacher could also exploit the intonation of question forms and the weak form of *do ...* if there was time.

LESSON 5
It'll Never Happen to Me !

The vocabulary in **1** serves as a warmer and links to the picture. You may want to do extra work on words such as *hic,mm,yummy,gasp* (and ask how they convey this meaning in their own language). The letter, in **5**, could lend itself to revision on the conventions of informal letter writing. It focuses on the functions of writing, and gives an opportunity for students to use actively the language of advice and also any vocabulary connected to food and diet studied in this unit.

LESSON 6
Confessions of Food and Drink Junkies

As a warmer, use the headlines as a lead into a brainstorm of vocabulary connected to addictions and discussion of any other students can think of (such as drink, drugs, gambling etc). Elicit what drugs are in Coca Cola and cigarettes. Instead of reading both texts students could read one each and exchange information on what they have read. Attention could be drawn to the styles of the two newspapers - with their emotive language and colloquial language. Students could be asked to imagine other situations where someone is addicted to something, and act it out. This could be followed by the writing of a newspaper report written in a similar style. The listening activity could be followed by a short summary of what Gillie said, written in the style of one of the newspaper reports earlier.

UNIT 3 EARNING A LIVING

This unit is based around the theme of work, and includes work in the home - by both men and women - and different attitudes to it. It also touches on unusual jobs as well as highly paid/stressful jobs and badly paid but socially useful jobs. Language areas suitable for revision would be comparative forms, adjectives and adverbs, modals of obligation, past habits and future plans.

Teacher's notes

LESSON 7
The Job or the Money?

The first activity lends itself very well to revision of comparative and superlative forms. It could be expanded into a discussion on the job students would most and least like to do. Prioritising is probably best done in groups. Activity **1c** lends itself to work on modals of obligation/absence of obligation. In **4b** students might well want to spend some time discussing the meaning of any unfamiliar vocabulary. **5** could be opened up into a discussion on the roles of men and women, and the opportunities available, if appropriate.

LESSON 8
Jobs with a Difference

A nice introduction to this lesson might be to elicit the words forensic pathologist by thinking of a case known to the students where a murderer was discovered in this way. They could also be asked a series of questions about what clues are found to convict a killer. The first listening (**1b**) is just for gist. The second time (**1c**) it may be better to stop the tape to give students the opportunity to answer the questions. Before reading the text (in **3**) elicit what students regard as 'glamorous jobs' and the possible disadvantages of these jobs. The adjectives in **5** lend themselves to work on pronunciation and stress. A natural extension might also be (near) synonyms/antonyms.

LESSON 9
A Job or Family Life?

Before reading the text you could write one or two of the quotes from the text up on the board, and ask students to predict who they think said it (by looking at the photos of the three women). They could be encouraged to give their own views on the quotes and/or predict how life and opinions will have changed over the generations. After reading the texts, in **3**, try to encourage students to give a summary of what the text said, rather than reading directly from the text itself. **4** could be developed into a discussion on the advantages and disadvantages of life for a woman in Rose's day compared with Cathy's life. It could lead to a discussion or survey on students' plans for the future, regarding work, marriage etc. There is potential for oral or written revision on past tenses, past habit (used to/would) in discussing the women's life in the past. The listening, in **8**, could be followed by a full scale discussion on how the role of men has changed, if at all, over the last fifty years, and how society views 'househusbands'.

UNIT 4 THE UNEXPLAINED

This unit centres on the paranormal and ranges from ghosts and the supernatural to Near Death Experiences. There is a full scale debate in Lesson **12**. Again, there is plenty of scope for work on narrative forms, and Lesson **12** lends itself to functional work in the area of giving opinions, and disagreeing.

LESSON 10
The Paranormal

The vocabulary activity on fear and surprise in **1b** could be extended out of the text to include a range of verbs and adjectives which could come up later in the speaking and writing activities. The speaking activity in **2** is a speaking activity in its own right, and also the lead-in to the listening. **1** could be done orally in groups, or as a written activity. Encourage students to include the vocabulary of fear in their stories. The reading in **6** could be done as a jigsaw reading activity, with groups of four students reading one text each. This unit again lends itself to remedial work on narrative tenses and linking words.

LESSON 11
Out of Body Experiences

A suitable beginning to this lesson might be to ask students if they have ever had any experiences when they have felt 'apart from their body' or in a different world. The picture in **1** and the words in **2** are also meant to serve as a warm-up and introduction to the topic. The listening task in **3** requires intensive listening, so it might be better to stop the tape after each extract to enable students to fill in the gaps. Again, it could also be done as a jigsaw listening task. In the reading activity, (**4**), students may want to make a note of any new vocabulary which comes up.

LESSON 12
Debating the Issue

If the class is reasonably small (12 and under) this can be done in two groups - as suggested. If you have a much larger group, there could be four or six groups instead (with two or three of the groups attacking and two or three defending the motion). An alternative way of running the debate, if the class is too large, is to have it in pairs instead of groups - so that each person who did the preparation in Group A pairs off with somebody in Group B. As a preparation for the essay for homework, in **3** encourage students to work together and organise their notes under the headings, as suggested. Remind them of suitable opening and conclusions for a 'for and against' essay, and give them help in connecting their ideas together logically.

UNIT 5 THE UNCONSCIOUS MIND

The theme of this unit is unconscious signs, which reveal something about the personality of the person concerned. Areas covered are doodles, sleep and dreams. The main language focuses on vocabulary to do with personality and gives an opportunity for work on synonyms, antonyms and connotation, as well as stress and pronunciation.

LESSON 13
The Unconscious Mind

An alternative 'warmer' would be to show students an example of one of your doodles, and get them to predict what this says about your personality. The first stage of the reading (**2c**) is meant to be skimming very quickly, so set a time limit and make sure that students don't expect to understand every word. **1c** could be expanded to a discussion on what the differences are between your personality and the definitions (using linkers of contrast. **Example** *It says I'm shy, whereas really I'm ...*). **3** is an exercise on word formation and could be made into a 'using the dictionary' activity. The exercise also includes a word stress exercise (and could include work on how the dictionary deals with word stress) and also connotation (**e**) - a very important area at this level and one which is picked up again in the next lesson.

LESSON 14
To Sleep ...

The short quiz is a warmer and aims to introduce students to the topic. The reading passage in **2** again focuses on vocabulary of personality. Encourage students to add any new vocabulary to their list in this area. The passage in **3** introduces the theme of dreams, which is taken up again in more detail in the next lesson.

LESSON 15
... Perchance to Dream

This lesson could begin with a brainstorm or class survey of what kind of dreams people have and discussion of possible interpretations. The aim in **1** is again on gist reading, which leads (in **2**) to reading for more specific information and for deduction of meaning in **3**. The listening texts in **4** could be done as a jigsaw listening, with 4 groups each listening to a different text. This could then lead into group work with the other three people in the group telling the fourth what the dream says about him/her, and giving advice on what he/she should do (based on the reading texts at the beginning of the lesson).

UNIT 6 YOUNG PEOPLE TODAY

The theme of this unit is young people; their values and aims and their way of living. It gives an insight into the life of teenagers in Britain in the 1990s and contrasts it with teenagers' lives in other parts of the world. Relevant language work would be revision of the present simple, the language of surveys (most, the majority, hardly any etc), connectors of contrast and concession (however, whereas, although) and the conventions of direct and indirect speech.

LESSON 16
Hopes for the Future

The initial prediction activity in 1 aims to give students a reason for wanting to read the article, as well as providing an opportunity for speaking practice. The activity in **1c** checks that students have understood the main point of each paragraph, as well as providing practice in question forms and giving a basis for the interview they will do later (in number **5**). The activity in **2b** requires students to look carefully at how the text is organised in preparation for their homework task later. Draw their attention to words and expressions such as *most, 65%, a majority* etc. - language which will be very useful in many of the other surveys done in this book.

LESSON 17
Teenagers Now

The points for discussion in **2** could also be used as a stimulus for debate if preferred. Encourage students to give their own opinions and agree and disagree. The creative writing activity in **5** could also be done first as an oral activity, with the actual writing being done at home.

LESSON 18
A Question of Class?

The first activity should be done in small groups. A possible follow-up could be for one member of the group to report back, using expressions such as *most of us, hardly any of us, none of us*. etc. The reading text is quite long and could perhaps be given to students to read at home before the lesson. The work on the text could then be compared in groups, so that students can help each other, before splitting into pairs to exchange information. The text is full of colloquial language. Students should be made aware of this aspect of informal spoken and written language and the conventions for marking colloquial language and slang in the dictionary. Encourage them to keep a note of this new colloquial language. **5** touches on the subject of the class system in Britain, and could be expanded into a longer discussion if relevant. An alternative to making notes, in **6**, would be to record the interview on a cassette player, and write a summary from the recording. Draw students' attention to the mix of direct and indirect speech in the texts and do any relevant work on the punctuation of direct speech in preparation for the writing task.

UNIT 7 A TROPICAL PARADISE?

The theme of this unit is places and travel, and the language element focuses on the description of places in different styles - from factual to persuasive language. There is a full scale roleplay in Lesson **21**.

LESSON 19
Describing Places

The brainstorming activity in **1** is to get students to think of descriptive words for a place. It would also be an idea to brainstorm possible categories of things one could write/talk about when thinking of a place (before they look at the categories in **2** and **3** below).
Try to elicit what features of the styles in **4** show that the extract comes from a particular type of reading text. In **5** encourage students to use dictionaries and to use exaggerated language and perhaps intensifiers (incredibly azure sky etc).

LESSON 20
Selling Tourism

Play the first part of the listening and get students to write down or mark on the map where Sarah went in Bali (make sure they have looked at the map first as the place names will be unfamiliar). The activity in **4** could be turned into a kind of competition to find the most attractive place. You may like to do some work on formal letters before giving students the homework. Make sure students know how to open and close a formal letter, and brainstorm ways of complaining.

LESSON 21
The Future of the Island

The listening in **2** is important input to the roleplay which follows. The situation for the roleplay and the people who will be at the meeting should be explained to students before they sub-divide into groups to prepare what they will say. Encourage them to include their own ideas as well as the ones on the rolecard, and make it clear that they must not read aloud from the card.

UNIT 8 EDUCATION

The theme of this unit is education and the three lessons cover school issues, and different kinds of schools as well as university education. The aim is for students to contrast their own system of education with the system in Britain and could lead to some form of project work such as a contrastive study of education (in schools or further education) in Britain and the student's own country. Remedial language work could focus on the language of likes and dislikes with the gerund, modals of obligation and absence of obligation, wish for regret and the 'past conditional'.

LESSON 22
Describing Schools

The opening activity might be an opportunity to talk a little bit about state comprehensive education in Britain and compare it to the old system of academic selection. Make it clear that public schools and boarding schools and (usually) alternative schools are outside the state sector and require the parents to pay fees. You may want to open this up into a discussion about the advantages and disadvantages of this kind of private education. There is scope in **3** for work on *not allowed to, have to, don't have to* and this could lead to a discussion of the rules at the various schools the students go/went to.
School uniform and mixed (co) education in **5** might not be an issue for all students, but they might be interested to think of all the arguments for and against, and present them in number **6**. The essay is the natural follow-up and gives more practice in organising a 'for and against' essay.

LESSON 23
Discussing Lessons

Explain that primary schools are for children between the ages of 5 and 11 and elicit what kind of things children of this age like and dislike at school, in order to motivate students to want to listen. There is potential in the listening text for remedial work on gerund forms and the vocabulary of likes and dislikes. The reading and listening extracts which follow touch on other issues relevant to schools. There is scope in number **6** to highlight features of natural spoken language such as fillers (*sort of, you know*) clarification (*I mean*) and other idiomatic language (*I reckon*).

LESSON 24
University Life

The reading and listening activities in this lesson give insights into some aspects of life at university in Britain which students may want to compare to their own. There is a particular focus on the aspect of living away from home and becoming independent, which students might like to discuss. The texts provide practice in the skills required to read texts efficiently, as well as vocabulary work.

UNIT 9 PETS AND WILDLIFE

This unit is based around animal life and the way we treat animals. It looks at zoos, the preservation of wildlife and also the peculiarly British obsession with pets. Language work could include narrative tenses, prediction about the future, the passive and phrasal verbs.

LESSON 25
A 'Good Day Out' at the Zoo

As an extension of the warmer in **1** you could also get students to categorise animals (under, for example, birds, reptiles, cats, etc.) This lesson could also lead to a debate on zoos, and it could also be extended to include a discussion on circuses.

LESSON 26
A Strange Obsession?

The opening texts put into focus some people's total devotion to animals, and lead to a discussion (in **b**) which could be expanded into a debate as to whether pets are often treated better than we treat our children. The reading text in **3** could also be exploited for narrative tenses, the passive and the style of diary writing. Some of the phrasal verbs and idiomatic language included in the text are exploited in **4**.

LESSON 27
The Animals We Might Lose Forever

This lesson focuses on scanning the text to find particular information, and work on vocabulary, in the form of a word quiz. It could lead to a discussion on animal experimentation and/or vegetarianism and the wearing of fur. An extra activity would be for students to make a poster or write a leaflet persuading people against a particular form of exploitation. They could also present these to the class, along with short talks to accompany them. There is potential here for work on prediction (*if we don't ... the animals will/may/might ...*).

UNIT 10 BRIBERY AND CORRUPTION

The last unit, like the first, is based around a short story - this time by Ruth Rendell - called *Bribery and Corruption*. Again, the aim is for students to develop reading and listening skills, extend their vocabulary but also to give plenty of stimulus for speaking and writing. Relevant revision areas of language could include conditional forms, criticism (*should/shouldn't have done*) and reporting verbs and tenses.

LESSON 28
Bribery ...

A starting point to the lesson could be to ask students what kind of restaurants they like eating out at, or show them pictures of different types of restaurants and ask them which they prefer. As they read the first extract they might want to make a note of the most difficult vocabulary. Before looking at the second extract ask students to predict what sort of food will be on the menu. There is an opportunity here to do some extra work on the vocabulary of food and drink. There is quite a lot of scope in **6** to do some more vocabulary work.

LESSON 29
... and Corruption

An extension of the reading in **1** would be to ask students what they would do/have done in this situation, and whether Nicholas was right in feeling he was being corrupted. Students could be encouraged to describe Sorensen, based on what we know of him up to now, and based on a description of his office (in **2**).
Encourage students to report the correct story (in **4b**) as accurately as possible.

LESSON 30
Revenge!

Get students to discuss their stories in groups before reporting back on the best one.
The last part of the story lends itself to a discussion of the moral issues involved and what Nicholas should/shouldn't have done. Some revision on reported speech and reporting verbs (*he explained/insisted* etc) might be useful input to the homework activity.

Key

UNIT 1 MURDER!

LESSON 1
'I've got something to tell you.'

1. **a** Possible answers: calm; loving; happy; smiling.
   b Yes. She looks forward to him coming home and is happy to be expecting a baby.
   c Soft mouth large dark eyes translucent skin.
   d He comes home by car punctually at around 5pm, his wife takes his coat and gives him a drink which he has sitting in his usual chair.
   e Possibly a stressful job, since he is tired.
   f Possible answers could include: reliable, predictable, thoughtful, relaxed.
   g Warm, clean, drawn curtains, table lamps alight, drinks on the sideboard.
   h Open answer. Possible answers are cosy, homely, comfortable.
2. **a** sideboard **b** glance **c** tranquil/placid.
   d slam **e** tinkle **f** content
3. **a** T **b** T **c** F **d** T **e** T
5. **a** Open answer (most likely one is that he is leaving her for another woman).
   b She is 6 months pregnant and shouldn't get upset.
   c He doesn't want her to talk about it and cause any scandal.
6. **a** He is dead.
   b Very upset sobbed weeping hysterically crying.
   c The men worked with Patrick.
   d Jack Noonan and O'Malley.
   e A small patch of congealed blood.

LESSON 2
'Don't make supper for me. I'm going out.'

2. **a** T **b** F **c** F **d** F **e** F
4. **a** It was wrapped in paper.
   b She carried it upstairs.
   c She swung the big frozen leg of lamb high in the air.
   d She stepped back.
   e He remained standing there…gently swaying.
   f Then he crashed to the carpet.
   g She stood for a while blinking at the body.
5. **a** i e ii d iii a iv f v c vi g vii b viii h
6. **a** That she was going home as usual to cook supper and if she found anything unusual at home it would be a shock.
   b She was humming a tune, smiling and calling her husband's name.
   c She felt shocked and upset.
8. Name of victim: Patrick Maloney
   Name of person who found him: Mary Maloney
   Relationship to dead person: Wife
   Approximate time of death: Between 5.55 and 6.10
   Place of death: in the living room of his home
   Cause of death: Probable murder
   People who visited scene after death: Noonan; O'Malley, a doctor; two detectives; a photographer; a fingerprint expert.

LESSON 3
'Get the weapon and you've got the man.'

1. **a** To get some vegetables for supper, as Patrick was too tired to go out.
   b To go and speak to the grocer.
3. **a** a corpse/a stretcher
   b to go to her sister's house/to go to his wife/to lie down on the bed upstairs. He probably said 'Why don't you…', 'Wouldn't it be a good idea….?', 'Hadn't you better….?.'
   c to put somebody up.
   d to see what happened.
4. **a** T **b** T **c** F **d** T **e** T
5. **a** a gun **b** a knife **c** an axe **d** a pillow
   e poison **f** a fist **g** a rope
6. **a** to have a drink **b** the meat in the oven **c** eating it
   d big/easy to find **e** on the premises

UNIT 2 HEALTH AND FITNESS

LESSON 4
You Are What You Eat

1.
Dairy food	yoghurt
Fish-oily	sardines
white	sole
Meat: red	lamb
poultry	duck
Vegetables: green	cabbage
pulse	beans
Fruit: fresh	grapes
dried	prunes
Confectionery	biscuits
Cereals/bread	pasta

3. **a** ii barbecue iii boil iv poach v roast vi stew
   vii grill viii casserole
6a
i	3
ii	4
iii	1
iv	5
v	1

LESSON 5
It'll Never Happen to Me!

1a eat: nibble, gobble, devour, munch, chomp
   drink: gulp, sip, knock back
   sleep: doze, nap, snooze
3. **a** double **b** heavy **c** binge **d** trim **e** brisk **f** switch
4. **a** Stay slim, get or keep fit, avoid too much stress, give up smoking, have a healthy diet and keep alcohol under control.
   b By exercising.
   c It raises the blood cholesterol level.
   d Relax with calming hobbies.
   e Because it strengthens the heart and lungs, and lowers blood pressure and cholesterol levels.
   f Cut down on fat and salt intake, eat more chicken and fish and lots of fibre, and grill rather than fry food.
5a **i** a friend
   ii James's heart attack
   iii a thankyou letter and an invitation to stay

LESSON 6
Confessions of Food and Drink Junkies

2. **a** 40 **b** £70 **c** when he was in court
   d shaking, he's hungry and can't sleep **e** £26 a week

Key

f at 12 **g** the influence of his friends **h** she didn't know **i** he pretended they were for someone else **j** He started shaking and sweating and was angry, tense and unreasonable
3   **a** knocks back **b** resorted to **c** plight **d** came to light **e** overdose **f** has ruined his life **g** His friends tried to force him **h** He was afraid of being left out/being the only one who didn't smoke **i** The amount of the drug he had to have every day
7   **a** chocolate/coffee
    b edgy and nervous/ attacking them
    c thicker/stronger/sleeping
    d her children's chocolate/many an argument
    e dependent/acupuncturist/recommended
    f to stop the addiction
    g sixteen pounds

UNIT 3 EARNING A LIVING

LESSON 7
The Job or the Money?

2a the first person = picture **3**
    the second person = picture **6**
2b
PAM
Likes   meeting nice interesting people
Dislikes the anti-social hours and shift work, the late hours, tired feet, headache, backache.
HAG
Likes   the variation of the job
Dislikes the difficulty of being paid when you don't know what to do
2c **i**   the hours the pubs are open
    ii out of usual working hours
    iii a period of work
    iv a boring person who sits at the bar
3a **i** patient **ii** ward **iii** shifts
4a **i** 4 **ii** 6 **iii** 2 **iv** 7 **v** 1 **vi** 3 **vii** 5
4b **i** F **ii** F **iii** T **iv** T
6b **i**   he buys and sells currency
    ii the travelling
    iii backstabbing and competitive
    iv they drink
    v   20 years

LESSON 8
Jobs with a Difference

1 c **i**   take photographs
            police the area
            wall off the area
    ii 2-3 hours
    iii time
            weapon
    iv if it was homicide or an accident, so that they can organise a manhunt if necessary
    v   to see if a murder was involved
    vi when young parents and (especially) children are involved
3b **i**   she needs to check the resort and she takes group of travel agents out
    ii trips to exotic countries, 5 star hotels, good food
    iii hard work, jetlag, staying alone in hotels
4   the media: journalist, news-reader
    travel: air-hostess, travel agent
    beauty or fashion: hairdresser, model
    counselling: psychoanalyst, social worker
    finance: mathematics,
    technology: accounting
    the arts: dancer, actor
    selling: estate agent, sales representative

LESSON 9
A Job or Family Life?

2

	Rose	Gladys	Catherine
Age	95	72	20
When they left school	13	14	?
Jobs	servant/cook, cleaner, housekeeper	milkmaid shop assistant	draughts-person
Hours/money	£1 per month began at dawn	5 shillings 8.30am-9pm	? begin 7.30
When did she stop work?	when she got married	when she got married	
Attitude to being at home	didn't miss work	never bored	will continue her career
Believe in equality?	Women shouldn't do some jobs	Man should be be head of family. Not sure about equality	Women are equal to men.
Working mothers	Women should look after children	Women miss out on pleasure of bringing up children if they work	Would return to work when kids are 3-4

6 b   **i** F   **ii** T   **iii** F   **iv** T   **v** T

UNIT 4 THE UNEXPLAINED

LESSON 10
The Paranormal

1 a **a** the figure of a man
    b a woman
    c Nuala's (dead) mother
    d A woman appeared in front of his car, telling him to go away.
    e Her father's new wife's nephew
    g terrified, froze with fear, deathly white, stared in horror, frightened
        shock of my life, panicked, amazed, couldn't believe her eyes
5   **a** ii **b** i **c** iii

LESSON 11
Out of Body Experiences

3a **i**   he had a heart attack
    ii   human shapes
    iii upset at returning
    iv   having a baby
    v   a light/great joy
    vi   of her baby/to help others
    vii down a tunnel
    viii Music, colours and her relatives and friends
    xi   to go back
4a vi, iv, i, ii, v, iii,
4b 6, 2, 5, 4, 1, 3

Key

UNIT 5 THE UNCONSCIOUS MIND

LESSON 13
The Unconscious Mind

2c 1 d 2 f 3 e 4 c 5 b 6 a
3a i b ii c iii d
3b i suspicion, jealousy, unhappiness
ii warmth, care, spontaneity
iii balance, observation
3c i f ii e iii c
3d i angry, pessimistic, creative
ii consistent, careful, logical, loyal, devoted, reliable, dull
iii spontaneous, warm
4 A 2 B 3 C 1

LESSON 14
To Sleep ...

2a i 3 ii 1 iii 4 iv 2
2b i 3 ii 1 iii 2 iv 4

a drowsy/light sleep/deep sleep
b 90 minutes
c Rapid Eye Movement, when your body is relaxed, but your brain is buzzing, 10-30 minutes.
d During REM.

LESSON 15
... Perchance to Dream

2 a 3 b 1 c 2 d 4
3 i gloomy ii buried iii sink iv leaking v pick upspeed vi grasp vii drab viii sparkle

UNIT 6 YOUNG PEOPLE TODAY

LESSON 16
Hopes for the Future

1c i What job do you want to do? (para 1)
How much do you expect to be earning by the time you're 30? (para 1)
Where would you rather go on holiday? (para 1)
What do you like watching on television? (para 1)
What would your ideal evening be? (para 2)
What sports do you like doing? (para 2)
Which famous person would you most like to be? (para 2)
Do you think you'll be married with children by the time you're 30? (para 2)
What issues are most important to you? (para 2)
2 a cosy b on the town c look forward to d ratings e issue
3b social life - 4 marriage - 6 family life - 1
smoking and drinking - 5 music - 3 clothes - 2
3c i F ii F iii T iv T v F vi F vii T

LESSON 17
Teenagers Now

1a i T ii T iii T iv T v T
3 going out with friends
where she'd go when she went out
drinking and smoking
wearing clothes
wearing makeup
freedom of teenagers today
relationship between parents and children

LESSON 18
A Question of Class?

2a EMMA 1 education/aims for the future
2 social life/hobbies/friends
3 relationship with parents/boyfriends and marriage
4 clothes/TV
5 TV/newspapers/politics
6 dream holidays/dream homes
7 English people
8 the future
SHARON 2 ambitions
3 education/boys/marriage
4 boys/marriage
5 social life
6 clothes/hobbies/TV/newspapers/hobbies
7 holidays
8 the future
3 EMMA a varied b on the whole c outlook d avid e well off
SHARON a dosh b loads c blokes d get rid of them

UNIT 7 TROPICAL PARADISE?

LESSON 19
Describing Places

2 i i ii d iii c iv g v a vi h vii e viii f ix b
4 i B ii C iii A

LESSON 20
Selling Tourism

1
Where she went	What she did there
Sanur	stayed in a hotel
Denpasar	visited the town
Singaraja	visited the town
Mt. Agung	went for a walk
Tanah Lot	saw the temple; took photos of sunset
Nusa Dua	went on the beach; had a massage
Kuta	went shopping at the market

2a Kuta beach is not unspoilt.
A part of the hotel was a concrete tower.
The swimming pool was small.
It was dangerous to swim in the sea because of the sea urchins and coral.
It was difficult to sit on the beach because of the sand snakes.

LESSON 21
The Future of the Island

2 a Australia b Western Europe c communications systems d health e Indonesia f taxi g hotel owners h drugs i sun-bathing j crimes k theft l 22 m sell n offering me

78

Key

UNIT 8 EDUCATION

LESSON 22
Describing Schools

1a A comprehensive school is a state school and is open to students of all abilities.
An alternative school is usually fee-paying and has got a different approach to learning or to education.
A public school is fee-paying and there is usually an examination to pass before being accepted.
A boarding school is a school that you live at during the terms.

5 **a** 'it' is school uniform,'they' and 'them' are girls
   c Helen: Nobody likes wearing school uniform, although there are points in favour of it.
   Nicholas: It is better to have mixed education so that you learn to treat each other as normal human beings.

LESSON 23
Discussing Lessons

1a

	Damian	Thomas	Dermot
i	x	English, spelling poetry	English, poetry reading, spelling
ii	maths	maths	maths
iii	teachers uniforms	teachers uniforms	x
iv	sport, football	x	games, football listening to radio
v	don't mind	don't like	don't mind

5 a iii b vi c vii d i e ii f x g viii h ix i v j iv
6a i stream ii bright iii they can get held back
    d i because the oral part is only a small part of the exam

LESSON 24
University Life

1a i 7 ii 2 iii 5 iv 8
b   i F ii T iii F iv F v T
2   i snooze ii drawbacks iii overdraft iv grant v catered
3   i independence ii renting iii grant iv being able to live her own life v leaving home vi cook vii bills viii independence ix valuable x work xi parents xii go out too much and waste time

UNIT 9 PETS AND WILDLIFE

LESSON 25
A 'Good Day Out' at the Zoo

2a
Keith: likes
Judith: unsure
Chris: unsure
Karen: dislikes
John: unsure

2b **Arguments**
For: the animals are well looked after and well-fed
they give pleasure, and a desire to travel
they are fun if you take children
only chance for children to see them
they can help save endangered species

Against: the animals are in captivity/cooped up
it is cruel

3a i T ii F iii T iv F v T
3c i Nature programmes, models of animals, video, film, etc.
    ii Zoos often don't succeed in breeding and even if they do there are problems in returning the animals to the wild.
    iii She suggests that people spend the money conserving the animals in the wild.

LESSON 26
A Strange Obsession?

1a i slow lane ii take off
    iii A bypass iv newts v motorway vi protested
    vii hedgehog viii kiss of life ix floating
    x water xi ducks xii water
    xiii advertisement xiv birthday
2 b **Extract 1:** = Tina Turner
     Extract 2: = Princess Diana
     Extract 3: = Margaret Thatcher
3a i 6 ii 11 iii 7 iv 1 v 4 vi 5 vii 8 viii 10 ix 2/9 x 3
b   i an owl in a chimney stack
    ii a dog, because it wasn't housetrained
    iii 2 dogs, a cat and a tarantula spider
    iv a hedgehog
    v a horse
    vi a cat
    vii a cow
    viii a swan
    ix an old lady's dog
    x a monkey

LESSON 27
The Animals We Might Lose Forever

a the attack on forests, which meant they had no food or shelter
b after the war
c the blue whale
d meat, fats and oils
e Kenya, Zambia and Zimbabwe
f black
g tusks
h Asian/Indian
i 300
j They take their heads for trophies and their skins for rugs.
k They have constructed special reserves for them.
3 1 exploited 2 snared 3 vast 4 species 5 threatened
   6 crops 7 dwindled 8 doomed 9 prey 10 onslaught
   11 extinction 12 trade 13 slaughter

UNIT 10 BRIBERY AND CORRUPTION

LESSON 28
Bribery ...

1 a No. He usually dines in his rented room, or at a steakhouse, and doesn't take taxis.
   b Expensive/grand.
   c It was their first date.
   d Uneasy and worried about the prices.
   e Quite at home.
2 a asparagus, grouse, roast potatoes, red cabbage, runner beans, braised artichokes, strawberries, chocolate roulade.
   b vegetable soup and a pork chop.

      c roast grouse
4 **a** man **b** chairman **c** father **d** redundant
    e Julius Sorensen **f** hated **g** greeted **h** calculated **i** owed
5 **a** T **b** F **c** T **d** F **e** F

LESSON 29
... and Corruption

1 **b** Not very striking, plain.
    c He could not treat the Hawthorne family badly again.
2 **a** Send Sorensen a blank cheque.
    b Perhaps it wasn't intended as a bribe after all.
    c So that he wouldn't have to pay the money back but neither would he be corrupted either.
    d Very elegant, expensive, plush.
    e Uncomfortable, ill at ease.
4b **i** It was a woman he picked up in a bar.
    ii He said he wouldn't allow himself to be blackmailed.
    iii He was very emotional (His heart began to pound and blood rushed to his face).
    iv The cheque was for sixty-seven pounds.
    v He tore it up.
5 **a** He expected Nicholas to ask for more money.
    b Very distressed.
    c A mental illness.

LESSON 30
Revenge!

2 **a** F **b** F **c** F **d** F **e** F **f** F
3 **a** considering **b** tycoon **c** overcome with remorse
    d iniquity **e** witness
4 **a** between 8 and 10 p.m. on Tuesday.
    b He was at Potters with a young lady.
    c disappointed.
    d Nicholas had gone to Sorensen's office the following day.
    e to tell them what he and Sorensen had talked about.
5 **a** He was embarrassed to talk about being bribed.
    b They probably think Sorensen asked him to say he was there.
    c Nobody remembers him being at the restaurant.
    d 'Did you see Mr.Sorensen at Potter's on Tuesday evening?'
    e 'I didn't see him. Of course I didn't.'

Tapescripts

UNIT 1 MURDER!

LESSON 1
'I've got something to tell you.'

Activity 3

'Tired, darling?'
'Yes,' he said. 'I'm tired.' And as he spoke, he did an unusual thing. He lifted his glass and drained it in one swallow although there was still half of it, at least half of it, left. She wasn't really watching him but she knew what he had done because she heard the ice cubes falling back against the bottom of the empty glass when he lowered his arm. He paused a moment, leaning forward in the chair, then he got up and went slowly over to fetch himself another.
'I'll get it!' she cried, jumping up.
'Sit down,' he said.
When he came back, she noticed that the new drink was dark amber with the quantity of whisky in it.
'Darling, shall I get your slippers?'
'No.'
She watched him as he began to sip the dark yellow drink, and she could see little oily swirls in the liquid because it was so strong.
'I think it's a shame,' she said, 'that when a policeman gets to be a senior as you, they keep him walking about on his feet all day long.'
He didn't answer, so she bent her head again and went on with her sewing; but each time he lifted the drink to his lips, she heard the ice cubes clinking against the side of the glass.
'Darling,' she said. 'Would you like me to get you some cheese? I haven't made any supper because it's Thursday.'
'No,' he said.
'If you're too tired to eat out,' she went on, 'it's still not too late. There's plenty of meat and stuff in the freezer, and you can have it right here and not even move out of the chair.'
Her eyes waited on him for an answer, a smile, a little nod, but he made no sign.
'Anyway,' she went on, 'I'll get you some cheese and crackers first.'
'I don't want it,' he said.
She moved uneasily in her chair, the large eyes still watching his face. 'But you must have supper. I can easily do it here. I'd like to do it. We can have lamb chops. Or pork. Anything you want. Everything's in the freezer.'
'Forget it,' he said.
'But darling, you must eat! I'll fix it anyway, and then you can have it or not, as you like.'
She stood up and placed her sewing on the table by the lamp.
'Sit down,' he said. 'Just for a minute, sit down.'
It wasn't till then that she began to get frightened.
'Go on,' he said. 'Sit down'.
She lowered herself back slowly into the chair, watching him all the time with those large, bewildered eyes. He had finished the second drink and was staring down into the glass, frowning.
'Listen,' he said, 'I've got something to tell you.'
'What is it darling? What's the matter?'
He had become absolutely motionless, and he kept his head down so that the light from the lamp beside him fell across the upper part of his face, leaving the chin and mouth in shadow. She noticed there was a little muscle moving near the corner of his left eye.
'This is going to be a bit of a shock to you, I'm afraid,' he said. 'But I've thought about it a good deal and I've decided the only thing to do is to tell you right away. I hope you won't blame me too much.'

LESSON 2
'Don't make supper for me. I'm going out.'

Activity 5

She carried the meat into the kitchen, placed it in a pan, turned the oven on high, and shoved it inside. Then she washed her hands and ran upstairs to the bedroom. She sat down before the mirror, tidied her hair, touched her lips and face. She tried a smile. It came out rather peculiar. She tried again.
'Hullo Sam,' she said brightly, aloud.
The voice sounded peculiar too.
'I want some potatoes please, Sam. Yes, and I think a can of peas.'
That was better. Both the smile and the voice were coming out better now. She rehearsed it several times more. Then she ran downstairs, took her coat, went out the back door, down the garden, into the street.
It wasn't six o'clock yet and the lights were still on in the grocery shop.
'Hullo Sam,' she said brightly, smiling at the man behind the counter.
'Why good evening, Mrs Maloney. How're you?'
'I want some potatoes please, Sam. Yes, and I think a can of peas.'
The man turned and reached up behind him on the shelf for the peas.
'Patrick's decided he's tired and doesn't want to eat out tonight,' she told him. 'We usually go out Thursdays, you know, and now he's caught me without any vegetables in the house.'
'Then how about meat, Mrs Maloney?'
'No, I've got meat, thanks. I got a nice leg of lamb, from the freezer.'
'Oh.'
'I don't much like cooking it frozen, Sam, but I'm taking a chance on it this time. You think it'll be all right?'
'Personally,' the grocer said, 'I don't believe it makes any difference. You want these Idaho potatoes?'
'Oh yes, that'll be fine. Two of those.'
'Anything else?' The grocer cocked his head on one side, looking at her pleasantly. 'How about afterwards? What you going to give him for afterwards?'
'Well - what would you suggest, Sam?'
The man glanced around his shop. 'How about a nice big slice of cheesecake? I know he likes that.'
'Perfect,' she said. 'He loves it.'
And when it was all wrapped and she had paid, she put on her brightest smile and said, 'Thank you, Sam. Good night.'
'Good night, Mrs Maloney. And thank you.'

LESSON 3
'Get the weapon and you've got the man.'

Activity 6

'Jack,' she said, the next time Sergeant Noonan went by. 'Would you mind giving me a drink?'
'Sure I'll give you a drink. You mean this whisky?'
'Yes please. But just a small one. It might make me feel better.'
He handed her the glass.
'Why don't you have one yourself,' she said. 'You must be awfully tired. Please do. You've been very good to me.'
'Well,' he answered. 'It's not strictly allowed, but I might take just a drop to keep me going.'
One by one the others came in and were persuaded to take a little nip of whisky. They stood around rather awkwardly with the drinks in their hands, uncomfortable in her presence,

81

trying to say consoling things to her. Sergeant Noonan wandered into the kitchen, came out quickly and said, 'Look, Mrs Maloney. You know that oven of yours is still on, and the meat still inside.'
'Oh dear me!' she cried. 'So it is!'
'I'd better turn it off for you, hadn't I?'
'Will you do that Jack. Thank you so much.'
When the sergeant returned the second time, she looked at him with her large, dark tearful eyes. 'Jack Noonan,' she said.
'Yes?'
'Would you do me a small favour - you and these others?'
'We can try, Mrs Maloney.'
'Well,' she said. 'Here you all are, and good friends of dear Patrick's too, and helping to catch the man who killed him. You must be terribly hungry by now because it's long past your supper time, and I know Patrick would never forgive me, God bless his soul, if I allowed you to remain in his house without offering you decent hospitality. Why don't you eat up that lamb that's in the oven? It'll be cooked just right by now.'
'Wouldn't dream of it,' Sergeant Noonan said.
'Please,' she begged. 'Please eat it. Personally I couldn't touch a thing, certainly not what's been in the house when he was here. But it's all right for you. It'd be a favour to me if you'd eat it up. Then you can go on with you work again afterwards.'
There was a good deal of hesitating among the four policemen, but they were clearly hungry, and in the end they were persuaded to go into the kitchen and help themselves. The woman stayed where she was, listening to them through the open door, and she could hear them speaking among themselves, their voices thick and sloppy because their mouths were full of meat.
'Have some more, Charlie?'
'No. Better not finish it.'
'She wants us to finish it. She said so. Be doing her a favour.'
'Okay then. Give me some more.'
'That's the hell of a big club the guy must've used to hit poor Patrick,' one of them was saying. 'The doc says his skull was smashed all to pieces just like from a sledge-hammer.'
'That's why it ought to be easy to find.'
'Exactly what I say.'
'Whoever done it, they're not going to be carrying a thing like that around with them longer than they need.'
One of them belched.
'Personally, I think it's right here on the premises.'
'Probably right under our very noses. What do you think, Jack?'
And in the other room, Mary Maloney began to giggle.

UNIT 2 HEALTH AND FITNESS

LESSON 4
You Are What You Eat
Activity 5

OK, Now for the answers to our 'healthy diet quiz'. Take a pen or pencil and write down your score as we go along.

Number 1   If you got **a** or **b** you score 1 point. You should really eat some green leafy vegetables and some raw vegetables every day. **c** scores 2 points, try to include vegetables like spinach and frozen peas, which are high in fibre. If you ticked **d** you get 3 points. Remember, vegetables are not fattening, and they're full of vitamins and fibre.

Number 2   If you get **a** or **b** you can have 1 point. Again, you should eat fresh fruit daily, as it's full of vitamins and also contains fibre. **c** scores 2 points and **d** 3 points, try to make your life more fruity. You must be able to find some fruit you like!

Number 3   If you ticked a you get 4 points. This is too much! You don't need to give up meat altogether, but try to find some lower fat food - perhaps plan a couple of meals a week around vegetables. **b** 3 points. Why not substitute fish or chicken for one of the meat meals? **c** 2 points. If you're happy with this, fine. Make sure you're getting enough protein, iron and B vitamins from food such as wholemeal bread, fish and yoghurt. **d** 2 points. If you eat chicken and fish you're doing well. If you are vegetarian make sure you are getting protein and vitamins from eggs, cheese and yoghurt.

Number 4   **a** 1 point.Good, you're getting enough fibre. **b** 2 points. Good too, but try to add more fibre to meat dishes, by adding beans or other pulses. **c** 3 points. Try to find some recipe books which show you how to plan meals based on beans and lentils. Indian, Italian and Mexican food have lots of good dishes using pulses. **d** 4 points. If you don't like eating wholemeal bread, keep on eating the white bread. It does have some fibre.

Number 5   **a** 1 point. Fish, especially oily fish, is an excellent source of protein. **b** 2 points. Good - eat more! **c** 3 points. The fish is good, but there is too much fat. **d** 4 points. You are missing out on a very healthy food!

Number 6   **a** 4 points. You function much better if you eat breakfast, and this means you are less likely to have mid morning snacks. **b** 3 points. This is high in fibre and nutrients and better than sugary cereals. **c** and **d** 1 point. Good. Carry on!

Number 7   **a** 4 points. You are eating too many empty calories which contain no vitamins or minerals. You may have weight problems as a result. **b** 3 points. Try to cut down. **c** 2 points. Well done. **d** 1 point. Excellent - if you're telling the truth!

Number 8   **a** 4 points. You must change this or as well as having a weight problem you may also have a heart problem. **b** 3 points. A bit better, but not much. **c** 2 points. Try other methods of cooking - grilling, poaching, steaming. **d** 1 point. Good. Stay like that.

Score
The lower the figure - minimum 9, maximum 30, the healthier your diet!

LESSON 5
It'll Never Happen to Me !
Activity 4

ANNOUNCER: Not many people realise that in Britain there are more deaths from heart disease than anywhere else in the world. Nearly 200,000 people a year die from it -that's one every three minutes, and yet it is something which can be prevented. Dr Mason, the big question is 'How can we try to avoid a heart attack?'

DOCTOR: I always tell people there are basically six golden rules - you should try to stay slim; get fit, or keep fit; avoid too much stress in your life; have a healthy diet; keep alcohol under control - and, if you haven't done so already, give up smoking.

ANNOUNCER: Could you tell us why is it so important to stay slim?

DOCTOR: Well, for the simple reason that the heart has to work harder if you're overweight and leads to a rise in your blood pressure. Basically the heart will also wear out faster the more work it has to do. Being slim puts less strain on the heart and so take lots of exercise and eat sensibly and you'll lose those extra kilos. Drinking and smoking too much also often leads to high blood pressure. So cut down on cigarettes and alcohol. Give up smoking completely - just throw the packet away, and try not to drink excessively. Never binge, just limit yourself to a certain amount which suits you.

ANNOUNCER: And why is it important to be fit?

DOCTOR: Being fit means that the heart and lungs become stronger - it helps to lower blood pressure, and decrease the level of cholesterol in the blood. Aerobic exercise such as swimming, running, cycling and brisk walking all help - 20 minutes two or three times a week is enough - and it will also help you to lose weight and feel more relaxed. So there's a lot to recommend it!

ANNOUNCER: Why have heart attacks suddenly become so much of a problem in the last fifty years or so?

DOCTOR: Well, many people are of the opinion that life has become too pressurised, and it is certainly true that too much stress can lead to heart failure. Mind you, stress can also be good for you - one person's stress is another person's impetus to achieve things. But too much can raise the blood cholesterol level. Some people survive very well on stress - most at risk are people who are very aggressive or competitive and people who tend to get angry and impatient quickly.

ANNOUNCER: I suppose the obvious way to stop stress is not to work so hard and to take more exercise, as you suggested.

DOCTOR: Yes, relax more with calming hobbies such as gardening, reading or painting. Many people expect too much of themselves you know, so limit what you can do and don't take on too much. Oh. and instead of reaching for a drink, or a cigarette have a massage or go to the sauna. And, very important, don't bottle up your feelings - try to express yourself more and talk about your problems.

ANNOUNCER: And have you any tips on how we can eat well. Everyone knows that a good diet is very important for a healthy heart.

DOCTOR: It certainly is. Well there's a lot these days in the media about this, but the basic point I would stress for a healthy heart is to to cut down on your fat intake. Solid fat - the kind found in meat, eggs, butter and other animal products - helps to build up cholesterol in the bloodstream which can lead to strokes. So try to avoid the hard, solid fats found in cream, butter, eggs and so on and instead, eat soft or liquid fats, such as vegetable or corn oil, which are much better for you. And grill your food rather than frying it whenever you can. Also, try to eat more chicken and fish and lots of fibre - in bread, pasta and so on. And finally, watch you don't eat too much salt.

ANNOUNCER: Dr Mason, thankyou very much for coming into the studio.

LESSON 6
Confessions of Food and Drink Junkies
Activity 7

GILLIE: Oh yes, I've certainly got my addictions, that's for sure, but I'm getting a little bit better recently, but for quite a few years I was very heavily addicted to chocolate and coffee um, and it really was an addiction, as people on cocaine or heroin or cigarette smokers - this was an addiction - it was terrible!
I'd wake up in the morning and the first thing I would want would be a bar of chocolate and at least two cups of coffee before I even sort of ventured out of the house. It was really bad, and if I didn't get it - if I didn't get my chocolate or my coffee, I mean I could really feel the difference in me - I got edgy and nervous and I'd go hunting, and if I saw anyone eating chocolate it was almost as if I wanted to attack them to get a piece of their chocolate, and I noticed that my coffee was getting thicker and thicker and stronger and stronger all the time and consequently, I mean coffee is a stimulant so the result of that was I hardly ever slept. I mean, I'd be up at 3 and 4 in the morning drinking my coffee and searching chocolate bars out. I mean I was even guilty of stealing my children's chocolate, which was really bad - caused many an argument between me and my little girl, was me raiding her chocolate stack, but it was really bad.
And I started to realise just how dependent I was becoming so I ventured forward into medicine and I thought I'll try alternative medicine first, so I went to this acupuncturist who was recommended to me, who strongly advised me to stop the addiction and I'd paid £16 for that advice - I mean, it was something I was quite aware of before I went in and nothing much else happened from that experience.
And I remember walking out and thinking 'Gosh, I could've bought a lot of chocolate bars with the money I've just paid her.'
But I have - I've consciously made an effort so, I instead of before, where I must have drunk, as I said 30 - 30 plus cups of coffee actually, now I actually count my cups of coffee and I'm certainly cutting down and I'm managing to have tea instead of coffee, or sometimes a lemonade, or something like that. The chocolate's been a little bit harder than the coffee,

UNIT 3 EARNING A LIVING

actually, because I'm a great muncher. But I have managed to cut that down a bit.

LESSON 7
The Job or the Money?
Activity 2

PAM: Well, the worst part about it, of course is the anti-social hours - starting fairly early in the morning well, you see that now we've got these licensing hours all the day through we can, of course, work all the day through. Shift work comes into it - double shifts are very difficult because you have morning shifts, you finish in the afternoon, then you're back on again in the evening with a very short break in the afternoon. You work late at night, you have little sleep - you get tired, your feet hurt, your back aches, you get headaches. But the lovely part about it is meeting all the nice interesting people, who come into the bar, who sit at table, who talk to you and tell you all different tales - tell you a lot about their life, tell you lots about their problems er some things are nice, some people are boring, of course, you always get the bar bore - tend to steer clear of them. You also always find out who they are fairly quickly because people tend to disappear. But most people have got something interesting to say and most people come into the bar because they want to speak to somebody and they like the social way of life. That's the nice bit about it.

GILLIE: Why did you go in for this kind of job?

HAG: Because I wanted to do something that was creative, had use of the hands and also required some scientific skills. I like the variation, the fact that every job is different and that you never know what you're going to be doing next. The main thing I don't like is the difficulty of getting paid and

Activity 6

PAUL: Yeah, I work for Nat West bank in the dealing room. The job is really buying and selling currency - the job I actually do. I'm in charge of all foreign exchange that goes through Nat West branches. I like the job because it pays well. I get up at 6 o'clock every morning and jump into my suit and jump into the car and leave the house at 20 past 6 so there's the 20 minutes rush in the morning to get the train that leaves at half past 6, it's an hour on the train. Sometimes it's freezing cold and it's pretty packed as well. Coming home is worse because there's all the push and the shove of trying to get on the train and the trains never run on time. The earliest I will get home is about quarter to 7 and probably the latest is a quarter past 8 so it's a long old day.

BRUCE: What's the atmosphere like in the dealing room?

PAUL: Well, it's becoming in a way rather backstabbing - people are given targets now to make money and it's up to them to make their target otherwise they don't get their dealing bonus - the younger guys trying to stab the guy in the back to get his job. Everybody wants everybody else's job, if you like. Having said that, the reason I work in London - anybody who works in London will or should be getting on better than working locally. The reason people work in London in the first place is because they should earn more money - I'm motivated if you like by money.

BRUCE: And do the people show the effects of the stress?

PAUL: Yeah there's a lot of drinking that goes on I mean you hear about the drugs on a programme like Capital City and I've never actually seen it. I would imagine it goes on - the drinking certainly goes on.

BRUCE: And how long do people last in situations like this?

PAUL: Probably about 20 years then they either give up or go and do something else within the bank so I'm quite pleased I've got out of being a dealer.

LESSON 8
Jobs with a Difference
Activity 1

BRUCE: Now when you are called out to see a body can you tell us, what do you look for first of all?

PROFESSOR: Well I mean you - usually what happens is somebody's found dead and the police are informed and then the scenes of crime squad which walls off the area and does all that sort of thing, polices the area, takes photographs and so forth - they're there already and then I arrive - they usually call me out about 2 or 3 hours later, and my first job is to - not to put my hands on anything, I usually keep my hands in my pockets - just cast my eyes around and see what I can see and then fairly quickly to try and take the body temperature which one has to do in order to establish the time of death as best one can and then I what the police want me there for really is to examine the body and to say to them well this person's been shot or stabbed or something with - hopefully with this or that or the other type of weapon at some sort of time which hopefully I can compute, which I usually can't and that's all they want to know - I mean they often want to know is is this accident or is it homicide you know I've been to cases where it was thought that a young girl for example had been bitten by a dog - bitten to death and it turned out when I got there that she was actually riddled with stab wounds - they were not dog bites at all, so it does make a bit of a difference and then of course the police when they find out -when they're told what we all think - then they have to launch a massive manhunt and that's quite an expensive item so they don't want to put out 3 or 400 policemen and vehicles and God knows what else on a wild goose chase.

BRUCE: Is it always possible to determine the cause of death?

PROFESSOR: No, no, it's often very difficult. Usually of course, many factors combine to cause death you can't say precisely... I mean if somebody's got his head chopped off quite clearly he's bled to death - there's not much doubt about that - but quite often you get cases where somebody's been beaten and partly strangled and may have had an overdose of alcohol and so on - you've got all these factors taken together and you really don't know precisely why they died.

BRUCE: Do you ever find you get emotionally involved in a case?

PROFESSOR: Well, I think you do. You're bound to, actually - if the situation is particularly tragic, when you know a young parent is killed or something of that sort or even worse, when young children are killed and unfortunately we're seeing an increase in the number of children that are being killed not accidentally so called - being abused and dying and these are very disturbing cases and they're ones, ones which I find very sad making and it's very difficult at times to keep your impartiality, really, not to get too swayed by emotion.

BRUCE: And could you tell us the perfect way to kill someone?

PROFESSOR: I could do, but I won't.

LESSON 9
A Job or Family Life?
Activity 9

TONY: I used to look after the baby and do all the cooking and pretend I was working upstairs, and the work upstairs didn't get done - the writing.

IAN: Because the baby disturbs you?

TONY: I really thought, when Benjamin was born, that I'd be able to paddle him with one foot and work just while he was amusing himself. It doesn't work that way - they, or certainly he needed constant attention. So, for the 3 months I looked after him completely on my own. I got absolutely nothing done, and went partially insane - there's not a great deal of conversation you can get out of a 7 month year old baby - and my wife would come home in the evening and I'd be semi-insane, unreasonable, non-communicative, generally difficult - the food wouldn't be cooked, the house wouldn't be clean - the baby wouldn't be washed and I'd be in a mood.

IAN: So are you responsible also for all the - you do the cleaning, washing and cooking?

TONY: Yes, well, that has also changed. At one stage I was doing all the cooking, cleaning, shopping, also trying to earn a living, babyminding but some of that got thrown out of the water out of the window. So I handed over the babyminding to a nanny and I've just engaged a cleaner to clean the house so we now have a cleaner and a nanny, neither of which we can really afford, but it gives us time to sit round worrying about the money we haven't got. So I just do the shopping and the cooking now, as househusband. But an important element of being a househusband is that you have to be ready and half-dressed and exploitable up to 20 hours a day - that's very important.

IAN: But doesn't your wife get jealous about the amount of time you spend with the kid?

TONY: Sometimes, not very often though. Anne-Marie has to be outside - she has to be doing a job, she needs a structure to her life - which is going to an office. She travels a lot but she thinks, I'm not sure if it's guilt or real - that she'd like to spend more time with Benjamin - but the opportunity she gets she often finds very frustrating but spending a lot of time with a small child is extremely difficult.

IAN: And what do your friends think about it? Don't they think it strange?

TONY: Most of them think it's bizarre. They think, a few of them think I'm actually not working here when I'm here - that I'm dodging work - that I'm on the dole. A lot of people can't accept that I'm not terribly career minded. They don't love me any the less, but they often find it difficult to understand - some of them.

UNIT 4 THE UNEXPLAINED

LESSON 10
The Paranormal
Activity 3

NARRATOR: OK well.. er.. this story is about a bloke who was driving home one night, late at night..there was a very stormy howling gale and so on..anyway he was driving along and er..he suddenly saw this little girl by the side of the road and she flagged him down, so as far as he was concerned she was an ordinary little girl in a white dress and he stopped. He wound down the window and she said 'You must help me, you must come quick, my mother is very ill. Come and help me'. So he said 'OK get in'. She got in the car, she directed him and drove to where the house was and erm .. he got out , he knocked on the door...erm...there was no answer but he could see that the latch was sort of open so he went into the house and there he found this woman who was very very ill and erm...anyway he...he helped her and, you know, she recovered a little bit after a while and then she said to him 'How did you know, how did you know I was here? Who told you I was ill?' and he said 'Well your daughter did'. And she looked at him, she went a bit white, you know, and said 'I haven't got a daughter'. She said 'I had a daughter but my daughter died when she was a little girl' and he said 'Well maybe it wasn't your daughter...it was a little girl'. He described the girl. 'You know... sort of long fair hair and a white dress.' And so the woman said to him 'Come upstairs with me'. They went upstairs and they went into a room. There was a wardrobe. She said 'This used to be my little girl's room'. They opened the wardrobe and in the wardrobe they found this white dress, soaking wet.

LESSON 11
Out of Body Experiences
Activity 3

ANNOUNCER: They are called 'Out of Body Experiences' or 'Near Death Experiences' and they can happen to ordinary people in everyday situations or when people have been very ill and have nearly died. Studies have shown that one person in three has had a mystical experience similar to and including near death experiences. They feel themselves released from their physical bodies and feel as if they are floating and looking down on themselves. For some it is a frightening experience but others are left feeling peaceful and happy. On the line today we have three people who have been through a Near Death Experience. First on the line is Tom Ball from Manchester.

TOM: Aye, it were April 3rd - that's it - and I were walking along a cliff yeah and I had this heart attack - I fell over the cliff - 70 foot drop right down to the beach - and I found meself in the sea - me left side wouldn't move - I was paralysed, I suppose, and I were in that much pain, and I drifted in and out of consciousness and it seemed as though I were moving through a tunnel towards bright light and I saw human shapes but I couldn't speak to them. I felt very calm there's no doubt about that - there was no worry. And the next memory was of a terrible pain - I've never had a pain like that and I never want it again and the nurse was there beside me and she said 'Thank God you're back'. It was April 8th - April 8th! Doctors thought I would die - they started to operate and during this operation I had another NDE. I felt again just as though I were in that tunnel heading towards a light and the voice said 'This time you'll stay with us' but well, I dunno, then I was back in the hospital, crying because I didn't want to return you see from this lovely place. Today my life has completely changed. I'm happier and my wife says I'm less selfish and I visit the old and sick and I tell them about my Near Death Experience.

ANNOUNCER: Good, good, thankyou, Tom. Susan Johnson we've got on the line now. You'd just had a baby, is that correct?

SUSAN: Yes, that's right. I was having a baby by Caesarean section, in fact, and I found myself in total darkness. I actually thought I was dead and funnily enough I felt angry rather than frightened - I wasn't really frightened at all. I was worried, but about my baby and then, it was strange, really, I found myself flying towards a light which grew until it actually surrounded me and the anger was replaced by a feeling of - I can only really describe it as intense joy. I couldn't see anyone but I became aware of a presence and I knew it was God - a voice said 'you know who I am' and another voice said 'Hello Sue, glad to see you here' - it was my grandfather who had died two years earlier. Naturally I was very happy to see him but all the time I was worried about my baby and I said I wanted to return. So my grandfather asked me why and I remember I told him I wanted to rear my baby and then to help others. Well, I found then that I was back in the operating theatre hovering above my own body. The doctor went out of the theatre and I floated above him - it really did, it felt like floating and I heard him say to my husband that he had a son but there were complications. My husband telephoned my mother and I heard him say that she had a grandson but that I wasn't too good - she said 'Keep praying'.
Well later I repeated my husband's conversation to my mother and he just couldn't understand how I could repeat it as accurately as that.
Since I had my Near Death Experience my life is much better in fact - I live in peace now that I know that life continues when we die. I get a lot of pleasure in life from very simple things.

ANNOUNCER: Thankyou, Susan. And finally, let's hear from Jane Powis in Bristol.

JANE: Well, it happened when I was in hospital. They'd given me the anaesthetic for the operation and I drifted off and then, suddenly, I wasn't dreaming, I just went floating down a tunnel into into this bright light without shadow. All around me was this wonderful wonderful light and I could hear wonderful music and there were colours everywhere - yes, I saw marvellous colours, and I knew I was in a place of peace - everything was so peaceful and it felt so good. And then suddenly I saw all my relatives and friends who had died - they'd already gone - and they were waving and shouting and when I went towards them they shouted to me to go back 'No, no, go back, it is not your time yet' - yet I wanted to go towards them. And then I woke up and I found myself back in hospital.

ANNOUNCER: Not all experiences are good, of course. One patient said she'd seen a deep hole of swirling mists, where hands were trying to pull her down. She could hear wailing noises, full of despair and was sure it was hell! Another person described it as black, with lots of desperate people and, once again, the wailing noise. Goodness and badness don't seem to influence whether people have positive or negative experiences, but those who have had negative experiences may feel guilty and frightened. Well, so far scientists can't give a very clear explanation of these experiences - some believe it's caused by shortage of oxygen which occurs when a person is near death, but in that case, one would expect the experiences all to be different. In fact, they seem to follow a coherent pattern, as you can see from our 'real life experiences' earlier in the programme. If you have had a 'Near Death Experience' please contact me, Steve Redmond, here at Radio 529. We'd be delighted to hear from you.

UNIT 5 THE UNCONSCIOUS MIND

LESSON 13
The Unconscious Mind

Activity 4

EXPERT: This first doodle represents a ship and demonstrates a desire for travel to far away places. All doodles which are of any form of transport probably indicate that the person feels trapped and in need of a change and a change which will take them a long way from where they are now. It's usually expressed as a desire for travel but in some cases it is just a need for action of some kind.

The second doodle shows someone who is very analytical - someone who thinks things out very carefully. The doodle is a clever and complex structure, it also shows considerable intelligence and the ability to plan things in detail. On the negative side, however, I suspect this person is not a very warm person. He or she probably doesn't spend much time on relationships but is more interested in a career.

The third doodle is quite an interesting one - it definitely shows someone who has got a rather muddled mind, probably not a very rational thinker. This is demonstrated by the lack of any pattern in the doodle. However, this person is lively and likes to be active - any laziness makes the person angry or irritated. The pressure of the pen shows that the person has energy and wants to achieve his or her ambitions.

LESSON 15
... Perchance to Dream

Activity 4

Extract 1

I dreamt once ... I dreamt a recurrent dream for a week or so that I was in love with Princess Diana... er... I was out of the country at the time and I dreamed I was in London and I saw this beautiful woman in a car and I just followed her and after a while she turned into a house and I followed her into the house and when I actually got into the house I realised there were two men there and I turned round and I recognised one of the men and it was Prince Charles and then I turned to look at who the woman was and of course it was Princess Diana... and Prince Charles said 'What are you doing in this house? What are you doing here?' and I couldn't really... I had nothing to say and so he chased me out with a wooden spoon.

Extract 2

And I have another recurrent dream and this is quite a frightening one because I'm usually walking along and I suddenly find that I can't walk hardly .. I can just drag one leg after another .. it's as if you were trying to walk through treacle or something .. and I'm really trying to walk and I can't and and again it's something I realise I've had before and I think it must be .. I feel when I have this dream as if I'm really old as if I'm getting old .. it's a very frightening dream .. I hate it.

Extract 3

Yes, I've had, several times in the past I've had a dream which is beginning to haunt me now because I keep thinking back to it, again it was .. each time I have this dream it's a very similar sensation, I have a feeling of anxiety, getting to the railway station feeling that er .. time is running out, running with my bags, getting through the ticket barrier, running up the platform, and seeing the train pulling out, running as fast as I can and reaching out to the door of the train but unfortunately missing the train completely - and then I just watch the train go off into the distance and feel terribly sad and depressed and this feeling of sadness is much more powerful than I think it would be in real life. It's a very very .. it's a nightmare in fact. Each time I have this dream .. for me it's a nightmare which I don't think it would be in real life.

Extract 4

There's...there's one that I've got occasionally about death, it's difficult to explain, I...I'm in a house or inside somewhere, anyway and it's all quite dark and I know that somebody has died erm .. there's an atmosphere about the place and I can see people coming and going in different dreams .. there are more people or fewer people and they're obviously really upset about something and there's the feeling in the dream that I'm supposed to know who has died and I don't and so I don't know how sad I'm supposed to feel .. or whether I'm supposed to just sympathise or whatever and it's really panicky because everybody else assumes that I know and they keep looking at me or not looking at me .. keep looking at the floor and so on and I wander through the house looking to find out who it is that has died erm .. and I never do and I'm sure it's somebody that I'm supposed to know and react about.

UNIT 6 YOUNG PEOPLE TODAY

LESSON 16
Hopes for the Future

Activity 3

BEATRICE: Well what I have found that is different from life in Britain is that young people live with their parents until they get married and they have a deep respect for their families and for their parents and their relatives... erm... I should say they are family centre... they feel that their parents are the central point of their lives... er not only the parents I would rather say the family itself... they... they erm love their parents, and they respect their parents and they feel that the whole family is not only their parents but their relatives as well... erm... they listen to their grandparents, their granddad and grandmam play an important part in their lives. Well, erm in referring to clothes they don't adopt fashions, they dress casually and they are very conservative in clothes.

INTERVIEWER: When you say casually what sort of clothes do they wear?

BEATRICE: Jeans ... sweaters, jackets, sports clothes. Erm... they'd rather say it takes long for them to adopt fashions... for instance now they are starting to wear earrings .. whereas here they have been used for ages .. for a long time .. they don't wear bright clothes, brilliant clothes. Er yes they are very fond of music and I think they listen to the same kind of music that the British young people do.
INTERVIEWER: ...so American...

BEATRICE: Yes American and what is in fashion, I don't really know what they listen to .. but I find that they know all the bands and singers and musicians that are in fashion now here. Well they spend their spare times .. erm .. mainly at home .. they organise parties. As a matter of fact there isn't much to do .. because apart from the schools and two or three clubs and two or three cinemas young people don't have much to do there. Anyway they don't .. they are not bored they always find something to do .. they meet their friends, they organise parties, er they don't often go to discos er although they stay up later than they do here .. the parties generally finish by three in the early hours of the day but erm .. that is admitted by everybody and there is no danger .. they don't drink alcohol, they have soft drinks when they go to parties and they don't smoke so much as they do here .. I've seen young people smoking and that caught my attention .. it was something I noticed that in my country they don't start so early. They start getting interested in the opposite sex very early .. and they have long long long friendships, and in some cases they even get married afterwards, er marriage is still the end of a love affair, nobody would think of not marrying when they get of age .. well er .. the average age of getting married is twenty five - the mid twenties although now it's quite difficult to get married, they find it too difficult because they haven't got .. they have their housing problems and serious economic problems and so now fewer young couples are getting married.

LESSON 17
Teenagers Now
Activity 3

INTERVIEWER: Mrs Lawson, when you were a teenager how much freedom did your parents give you?
MRS LAWSON: Well, they wouldn't have allowed us - we had to always go out with somebody that they approved of, I mean even with girls, like - or that - we always had approval of them, we just couldn't go out like the way you can now, really, and, but they were very sensible, really - they didn't restrict you to that extent that you didn't get out - but they had to know where we were going, who we were going with and what time we were home.
INTERVIEWER: When you went out where would you go?
MRS LAWSON: Well it would be some social - there were no clubs or anything in those days - it would be chiefly to people's houses, mostly to houses really - friends that they approved of.
INTERVIEWER: Were you allowed to drink or smoke?
MRS LAWSON: No, definitely not. No, I don't think even if they were alive now would allow me to.
INTERVIEWER: Could you wear the clothes that you wanted to?
MRS LAWSON: Well, that always was a problem like. You did try to dress a little different - but on the whole they didn't, it wasn't too bad. But they had their own ideas.
INTERVIEWER: And make-up?
MRS LAWSON: In my early days there was no make-up. I don't remember doing make-up till I left home really . . . unless, a cream to keep your skin proper - but there was no lipstick or make-up of any description.
INTERVIEWER: So what do you think of the life of a teenager today?
MRS LAWSON: Sometimes I think it was just as nice when I was a teenager, although they have much more freedom. I think you can have too much really like I think parents still should talk to their children. I mean, I think it's nicer when parents and children are friendly, as one really, and talk to them and even you don't agree with them you talk as if you - in your little way you can let them see which is right and which is wrong, can't you? I think a lot of parents, they push their children away and they don't really enjoy them. I like children to be able to come to you if there's a problem and talk about it and you talk in their language like.

UNIT 7 TROPICAL PARADISE?

LESSON 20
Selling Tourism
Activity 1

INTERVIEWER: So Sarah, how was your holiday in Bali?
SARAH: Oh, it was fantastic - the best three weeks of my life I think (really) absolutely gorgeous .. really .. I don't know it was just so different from anything I've seen before, just really really exciting.
INTERVIEWER: Oh right and you recommend people to go there?
SARAH: Oh yes, I mean the flight's very very long, you have to be prepared to make the journey but oh it's just really worth it when you get there.
INTERVIEWER: So what's so good about it?
SARAH: Well the place is beautiful, I mean you really do have golden beaches, absolutely fantastic views, palm trees, the climate's nice, it's ..
- It's not too hot?
- It's very hot but there's .. well when I was there there was always a wind off the sea and that kind of cools you down, it's beautiful and then there's so many interesting places to visit, really these temples, there's a lot to learn about the religion and the beliefs of the people and then .. it's a land of contrasts really because you get the hotels which are very comfortable .. built for the tourists and then you go outside and you see life as it really is .. you know it's a great contrast between the two things.
INTERVIEWER: Right so where were you staying exactly? Can you show me on the map?
SARAH: Well yeah. We were staying here at Sanur which is near Denpasar the capital .. and we visited Denpasar .. you know early on.
- What's that like?
- Erm a kind of crowded city basically .. very chaotic .. we didn't really stay there very long because it was hot in the city so we preferred just to have like half a day there (yeah) and then we visited quite a lot of other places on the island .. erm one day we went up to the North to visit I think a town it's called Singaraja in the North .. we visited that and that was very different again from the South of the island .. erm .. we visited the volcano which is between Denpasar and Singaraja .. I don't know .. do you know it? .. I think it's called Mount Agung .. something like this .. yes.
INTERVIEWER: Did you what .. could you go to the top of what?
SARAH: Well we didn't .. we went for a walk .. we didn't go to the top .. erm .. the climate was just so different there. .. really erm stormy, these black clouds .. and you know very humid, very wet .. and the erm another day we went more to the West .. to the temple of Tanah Lot which is very famous, it's out on the seashore and everybody waits for the sun to go down and takes photos of the sunset behind the temple .. it's lovely there .. and another day we went down to the south to Nusa Dua where there was a beautiful beach and we had a massage on the beach there with some of the local people.
INTERVIEWER: Yeah, did you go to Kuta beach?
SARAH: Yes we did actually, we went to Kuta beach where we did a lot of shopping in Kuta because there's a big market .. the beach was a little bit .. there were too many people actually there.

- Well I've heard it's sort of spoiled there .. too many tourists and just set up for the tourists.
- Yeah I was a bit disappointed by that actually because in the brochure we read it said that Kuta was a really nice beach but when we got there I found it a bit disappointing .. I much preferred the other beaches.
- Yeah, was it a sort of package holiday you went on?
- Yeah, it was this package holiday, we looked through the brochures, we chose one company, and it was obviously the hotel included .. we had one meal in the hotel and then we did the tours on our own, we didn't stay with the company.
- But was the brochure accurate, I mean did it really say, you know did it tell the truth?
- Well .. I mean the hotel, in the brochure it had this picture of one part of the hotel which is really beautiful .. erm low kind of chalet type huts and a lovely swimming pool but in fact that's only one part of the hotel, they didn't show the kind of concrete tower which is the main part of the hotel so it was a bit disappointing when we first arrived I though 'oh no - if the hotel is like this I don't want to stay here' but luckily we were in the garden part so .. the pool too, I mean in the brochure it looks like this enormous swimming pool, it was actually quite small .. it was alright you know. We couldn't, I was a bit disappointed .. it said you could swim in the sea but .. in fact, when we went to the beach there were a lot of snakes on the beach, so it wasn't (snakes?) yes, those small kind of sand snakes so we couldn't really sit there and also in the sea they had a lot of sea urchins so you could swim but you had to be very very careful where you put your feet and it was quite dangerous with the coral because you could cut yourself quite badly.
- That was on Sanur beach (yeah) so you had to swim in plimsolls or ..
- Yes in fact we swam mostly in the pool and just kind of went to the beach .. we went out in a boat one day and that was nice but you know the brochure exaggerated a bit let's say.

LESSON 21
The Future of the Island

Activity 2

RADIO ANNOUNCER: For several years now there has been increasing concern in Indonesia about what is happening in Bali. Despite being a relatively small island in the middle of a huge archipelago it has, for some years, been a Mecca for large numbers of Australian tourists. In recent years Bali's fame has spread to most of Western Europe and the number of jets flying into Denpasar airport with its load of package tour visitors has increased dramatically. Of course this has meant more precious foreign exchange coming into Indonesia and riches for some entrepreneurs, especially shopkeepers, taxi drivers and hotel owners. In terms of infrastructure the tourist invasion has brought many benefits - better roads, an improved communications system, a better health service and altogether a higher standard of living than in the rest of Indonesia. But all is not rosy in the state of Bali. Not even this idyllic island with its gentle people and traditional culture has been able to escape coca cola imperialism and the muck it brings in its wake. The residents of this beautiful island are beginning to feel angry about the insensitivity of those tourists who sunbathe topless on the beaches of Kuta or Sanur, who ride their motor bikes late into the night, who slop around the town drunk on imported beer, who hunt out the Western style discos and the growing number of prostitutes who operate from the hotels or accost you in the street. The Indonesian police have reported a significant increase in the number of crimes committed on the island especially theft, mugging and prostitution. From reports of seizures at Denpasar airport it seems that the days of the gentle hippy looking for nothing stronger than a diet of marijuana or the local 'magic mushrooms' are over. The modern hippies get their kicks from much harder fare - opium and heroin in the main. Another import that the Indonesian is worried about is AIDS. How has all this affected the people themselves? In many cases the traditional third world welcome has been replaced by the aggressive hard sell. In some places it is difficult to walk more than a few steps without being accosted by someone wanting to take you somewhere in his car, by someone wanting to drag you into his shop or by someone offering you a fake Gucci watch. The popular beaches are the worst of all. I sat on Sanur Beach for one hour and was disturbed no less than twenty-two times by youths (probably playing truant from school) wanting to sell me something or by old ladies offering me a massage. Some tourists are still taken in by the glossy brochures with their pictures of deserted beaches, verdant rice terraces, exotic food and traditional lifestyle. Let's speak to someone else who's also been there.

TOURIST: We were expecting basically I suppose an island paradise, this is the impression that's created in the advertisements and the travel agent's blurb but we were rather disappointed in many respects. First of all the people tended to although they were outwardly very friendly, their curiousity so far as my daughter who was quite small and blonde was concerned was a little bit alarming to her, they wanted to sort of touch her hair .. I mean nothing threatening or anything like that but it was a little daunting as you can imagine for a six year old girl to have sort of people coming up to her and clucking in her face and wanting to touch her hair .. and also they had many things to sell, many nice things it's true but they were .. they got incredibly pushy and life actually became a bit of a hassle in terms of warding these people off because one shop is very like the next shop and they've all got very similar things and some very nice things as I say but we were really more interested in just having a look, just looking and making our choice depending on the moment rather than being pushed into it by the shopkeepers .. and they weren't easily put off .. that was the other thing .. they would pursue you down the street sometimes if you'd walk past a shop or if you were advancing towards their shop they would come up and try and pull you inside their shop it got a little bit trying .. you couldn't actually take a walk down the street without this happening and I think that got a bit too much for us in some respects .. especially if it was very hot and you know perhaps tempers could be easily frayed .. I don't think we actually lost our temper but it was sometimes a near thing ..
The general impression of the island was that it was very touristy at least the Southern part of the island, now I've heard the North is nice and very beautiful but the tourists tend to stick in two particular areas in the South, Sanur where we were and along the East coast, Kuta which is very full of Australians, it's a kind of package destination and erm .. very very crowded, very noisy, very dusty and pretty unrelaxing.

RADIO ANNOUNCER: It doesn't take long for opinions like these to go the rounds. Already Bali is getting a reputation for being the Asian version of the Costa Brava where people go abroad but take their country with them. Unless Bali can improve its image it will join a long list of places which have destroyed themselves by pandering to the demanding tourist.

UNIT 8 EDUCATION

LESSON 22
Describing Schools

Activity 5

HELEN: Well I don't, I suppose I don't like wearing it, but if you come to think of not wearing it you'd have to think what to wear each morning. Well, it does stop people, you know, from you know being horrible about other people's clothes but and it's quite expensive though in the long run, with the blazers and everything, but I don't, nobody really likes wearing it at all, no.

NICHOLAS: I think boys and girls, they tend to think of the opposite sex in a sort of a kind of a sort of a remote sense, not really sort of um well normal people. I mean, as sort of objects, but if they actually sort of grew up with them in a school environment they'd get to know them I mean just, and just realise that they're just like themselves.

LESSON 23
Discussing Lessons
Activity 1

Extract 1
I don't like some of the teachers because sometimes they blame you for something you didn't do, and I don't like the uniforms because you can't roll around in the mud or do sudden tackles in football really well and when you have to work when it's meant to be free time or games or something, that's silly as well. Even if you haven't finished, you can do it another day.

Extract 2
I don't like the idea of uniforms either and I don't really like having teachers - I just like to do my work on my own. Yes I would do it I'd make sure I'd get it done but I'd still talk. I don't like getting out of bed early because on Saturdays and Sundays I stay there till about 1 o'clock and I don't like maths - I do like English, spellings, poetry erm I wish I could do them all day as well 'cos I like them.

Extract 3
Well I don't mind getting up early because my radio turns itself on automatically and I like listening to that but when I get to school I'd like to do English or poetry and reading or spellings all day and then I like games and football and things and I don't like maths - no way.

LESSON 24
University Life
Activity 3

JUSTINE: I've been at university a couple of years now. I've really enjoyed it, the independence of it I think is the best thing. I went away from home and I'd never paid any bills before, I'd never had any responsibilities at all really, and I had to rent a house er budget my grant, work out how much I could spend each week, and that was quite a responsibility. The best thing was being able to live my own life, and do what I want. I mean, did you find that?

BEVERLEY: Yes, I think leaving home is the most important part, and you learn such a lot by doing that, as you say, doing everything for yourself, having to cook, look after bills which your parents would've done for you but it gives you such a strong sense of independence and having to cope for yourself, that I think it's a very very valuable thing to do.

JUSTINE: It's, I mean like going to parties you could come in whenever time you want and .. but also you've got to be quite responsible in the sense that the self discipline of making yourself work 'cause you've got no parents to make you do your homework - you've got to, you know, which is quite important.

UNIT 9 PETS AND WILDLIFE

LESSON 25
A 'Good Day Out' at the Zoo?
Activity 2

Extract 1
I like to see the animals there and most of the zoos there's usually in a fairly natural state .. alright some of them are not and I know that .. the good zoos usually have .. there's plenty of space, they're well looked after, they're well fed and I think that they probably give a great deal of pleasure not only to adults but to young children who've never seen these animals and may also give them some inkling to travel abroad.

Extract 2
Well, I don't really like going to zoos too much .. except with children, it can be quite fun when you take children, but um I think on the whole, I I think they have their points and I think the main advantage that I see of zoos is that it does allow endangered species to be at times protected, so that, and at times even that new animals can be born in zoos whereas they might not be able to be born in the wild so I suppose they do have that advantage but as I say I don't like them myself.

Extract 3
Well, I have been to a few zoos in my life .. I was .. I enjoyed going there when I was younger obviously as a child, now I feel it is a bit cruel to coop animals up in cages etc, but I suppose it's the only chance for youngsters etc to see such animals isn't it really?

Extract 4
If you ask me zoos have got to be one of the cruellest ways we've got of dealing with animals. I mean they are brought from other countries into a really cold place like ours, erm, they've got all these people staring at them all day, they've got no space in which to exercise, and it's just terrible and then we do this to animals and say that we're a nation of animal lovers .. it's ridiculous.

Extract 5
Well my first reaction is that I'm very much against them because I feel that the animals are being held in captivity and especially some animals like antelopes which love to run across the er the plains and savannahs of Africa and various other countries here .. here they are in often in large .. well near large cities and in quite confined spaces so I'm against them, but er I would like to add to that that recently I saw a programme on television about the Oryx from Oman, the Arabian Oryx which is a very rare animal and in fact it had completely died out in Oman itself and an American zoo had kept several of these, quite a few of these in captivity but had .. through this they were able to reintroduce them to the desert in Oman and so a species was saved in fact by a zoo, so I'm now reconsidering my opinion.

LESSON 26
A Strange Obsession?
Activity 2

Extract 1
Well, if this person were an animal I'd say she would be a big cat like a tiger, or maybe a puma erm because she's very sensuous uh she moves very gracefully and she's got a very strong, powerful voice.

Extract 2
Yes, it's difficult, isn't it? I think if she was an animal she would be a gazelle. Gazelles are slim, fast moving, very beautiful, young, and I think they're quite noble animals really.

Extract 3
If this person were an animal I think she'd be an alligator because she's cruel and efficient and aggressive and frightening.

Tapescripts

UNIT 10 BRIBERY AND CORRUPTION

LESSON 29
... and Corruption
Activity 4

Sorensen lit a cigarette. He didn't offer the box. He looked at Nicholas and moved his head slowly from side to side. At last he said:
'I suppose I should have expected this.'
Nicholas opened his mouth to speak but Sorensen held up his hand. 'No, you can have your say in a minute.' His tone became hard and brisk. 'The girl you saw me with last night was someone - not to put too fine a point on it - I picked up in a bar. I have never seen her before, I shall never see her again. She is not, in any sense of the word, a girlfriend or mistress. 'Wait,' he said as Nicholas again tried to interrupt. 'Let me finish. My wife is not a well woman. Were she to find out where I was last night and whom I was with she would doubtless be very distressed. She would very likely become ill again. I refer, of course, to mental illness, to an emotional sickness, but . . .'
He drew deeply on his cigarette. 'But all this being so and whatever the consequences, I shall not on any account allow myself to be blackmailed. Is that understood? I paid for your dinner last night and that is enough. I do not want my wife told what you saw, but you may tell her and publish it to the world before I pay you another penny.'
At the word blackmail Nicholas's heart had begun to pound. The blood rushed into his face. He had come to vindicate his honour and his motive had been foully misunderstood. In a choked voice he stuttered:
'You've no business - it wasn't - why do you say things like that to me?'
'It's not a nice word, is it? But to call it anything else would merely be semantics. You came, didn't you, to ask for more?' Nicholas jumped up. 'I came to give you your money back!' 'Aah!' It was a strange sound Sorensen made, old and urbane, cynical yet wondering. He crushed out his cigarette. 'I see. Youth is moralistic. Inexperience is puritanical. You'll tell her anyway because you can't be bought, is that it?'
'No, I can't be bought.' Nicholas was trembling. He put his hands down flat on Sorensen's desk but still they shook. 'I shall never tell anyone what I saw, I promise you that. But I can't let you pay for my dinner - and pretend to be my father!' Tears were pricking the backs of his eyes.
'Oh, sit down, sit down. If you aren't trying to blackmail me and your lips are sealed, what the hell did you come here for? A social call? A man-to-man chat about the ladies you and I took out last night? Your family aren't exactly my favourite companions, you know.'
Nicholas retreated a little. He felt the man's power. It was the power of money and the power that is achieved by always having had money. There was something he hadn't ever noticed about Sorensen but which he noticed now. Sorensen looked as if here were made of metal, his skin of copper, his hair of silver, his suit of pewter. And then the mist in Nicholas's eyes stopped him from seeing anything but a blur. 'How much was my bill?' he managed to say.
'Oh, for God's sake.'
'How much?'
'Sixty-seven pounds,' said Sorensen, 'give or take a little.' He sounded amused.
To Nicholas it was a small fortune. He got out his cheque book and wrote the cheque to J Sorensen and passed it across the desk and said, 'There's your money. But you needn't worry. I won't say I saw you. I promise I won't.'
Uttering those words made him feel noble, heroic. The threatening tears receded. Sorensen looked at the cheque and tore it in two.

'You're a very tiresome boy. I don't want you on my premises. Get out.'

LESSON 30
Revenge!
Activity 4

'It has been established,' said the Inspector, 'that Mrs Sorensen was killed between eight and ten pm on Tuesday.'
Nicholas nodded. He could hardly contain his excitement. What a shock it was going to be for them when he told them about this supposedly respectable businessman's private life! A split second later Nicholas was left deflated and staring.
'At nine that evening Mr Julius Sorensen, her husband, was in a restaurant called Potters in Marylebone High Street accompanied by a young lady. He has made a statement to us to that effect.'
Sorensen had told them. He had confessed. The disappointment was acute.
'I believe you were also in the restaurant at that time?'
In a small voice Nicholas said, 'Oh yes. Yes I was.'
'On the following day, Mr Hawthorne, you went to the offices of Sorensen-McGill where a conversation took place between you and Mr Sorensen. Will you tell me what that conversation was about, please?'

Activity 5

'It was about my seeing him in Potters the night before. He wanted me to . . .' Nicholas stopped. He blushed.
'Just a moment, sir. I think I can guess why you're so obviously uneasy about this. If I may say so without giving offence you're a very young man as yet and young people are often a bit confused when it comes to questions of loyalty. Am I right?' Mystified now, Nicholas nodded.
'Your duty is plain. It's to tell the truth. Will you do that?'
'Yes, of course.'
'Good. Did Mr Sorensen try to bribe you?'
'Yes.' Nicholas took a deep breath. 'I made him a promise.'
'Which must carry no weight, Mr Hawthorne. Let me repeat. Mrs Sorensen was killed between eight and ten. Mr Sorensen has told us he was in Potters at nine, in the bar. The bar staff can't remember him. The surname of the lady he says he was with is unknown to him. According to him you were there and you saw him.' The Inspector glanced at his companion, then back to Nicholas. 'Well, Mr Hawthorne? This is a matter of the utmost seriousness.'
Nicholas understood. Excitement welled in him once more but he didn't show it. They would realise why he hesitated. At last he said:
'I was in Potters from eight till about nine-thirty.' Carefully he kept to the exact truth. 'Mr Sorensen and I discussed my being there and seeing him when I kept my appointment with him in his office on Wednesday and he - he paid the bill for my dinner.'
'I see.' How sharp were the Inspector's eyes! How much he thought he knew of youth and age, wisdom and naivety, innocence and corruption! 'Now then - did you in fact see Mr Sorensen in Potters on Tuesday evening?'
'I can't forget my promise,' said Nicholas.
Of course he couldn't. He had only to keep his promise and the police would charge Sorensen with murder. He looked down. He spoke in a guilty, troubled voice.
'I didn't see him. Of course I didn't.'